INSTANT
BOOK WRITING
KIT

REVISED EDITION

INSTANT BOOK WRITING KIT

- - - - -

How To Write, Publish and Market Your Own Money-Making Book (or eBook) Online

REVISED EDITION

A Step-by-Step Success Formula

By Shaun Fawcett, M.B.A.

- - - - -

Find out <u>exactly</u> how I wrote, published and marketed a dozen successful books and ebooks while completely bypassing the traditional publishing model...

Library and Archives Canada Cataloguing in Publication

Fawcett, Shaun, 1949-
Instant book writing kit [electronic resource] : how to write, publish and market your own money-making book (or eBook) online / by Shaun Fawcett. -- Rev. ed.

Includes bibliographical references and index.
Also available in electronic format.

ISBN 978-0-9781700-8-0

1. Authorship. 2. Authorship--Marketing. I. Title.
HF5415.1265.F38 2008a   808'.02   C2008-901439-1

Final Draft Publications
1501 Notre-Dame West, Suite No. 5
Montreal QC, Canada H3C 1L2

http://www.WritingHelpTools.com

TABLE OF CONTENTS

Special Notes Re: Hyperlinks

Because this book was first created and published online as an eBook with "live" clickable hyperlinks throughout, those links have been displayed in their entirely in this printed version for your information. Even though those links are not clickable in this version of the book, they still provide pertinent website URL addresses that you can type into your Internet browser should you want to explore online for further information.

The hyperlinks are easily identifiable because they are underlined just as they would be on a website or in an eBook.

Dedication

This book is dedicated to the tens of thousands of aspiring self-publishers who have visited my writing help websites and read my various articles about how the ordinary person can create, publish and market their own books via online channels without being victimized by the traditional publishing model. I am especially thankful to those people who have purchased my books on the subject and used the information prescribed therein to publish their own books/ebooks.

PREFACE TO PRINT EDITION

Instant Book Writing Kit (Original Edition) was initially conceived, written and published as an ebook back in June 2004. Since that time, the eBook version has been available online for purchase and download from a dedicated website: http://www.instantbookwritingkit.com

That ebook version has also been available for purchase and download from numerous digital download distributor websites on the Internet.

In parallel with that, since late 2004 a print-on-demand (POD) paperback version of the book has been available for purchase through more conventional channels that distribute and sell conventional hardcopy books.

The three versions of this book (i.e. website version, digital download version, printed POD book version) are perfect examples of the "online publishing model" in action. That OPM is explained in detail later on in this book.

In fact, this multi-channel publishing and distribution of *Instant Book Writing Kit (Revised Edition)* is a living example of exactly what this book is all about.

As I mention later in the section on Online Distribution Channels, if you want to cover the broad needs of the entire book-buying market, it is essential that you also publish a print-on-demand (POD) version of your book/ebook, like this one. Many people still insist on having a hard copy book just like they get in the bookstores.

If you don't satisfy that more traditional market you will be leaving significant money on the table since these people won't accept digital substitutes, either because they don't understand them, or they just don't like using them.

INTRODUCTION

REVISED EDITION NOTES

The first edition of *Instant Book Writing Kit* was published as both an eBook and a paperback in 2004. Since then it has been a steady seller both from my websites and through various other channels, which I will discuss in detail later on.

I have received e-mails from scores of people who have purchased the original book telling me how much it has helped them on their journey to create and publish their own book/ebook. People who have bought the book seem particularly impressed with the practical step-by-step nature of the material.

I probably could have waited another year or two before updating and revising this book. In fact, based on a careful review of the book contents that I just did in preparation for the revisions, I would say that more than 95% of the information and resource links in the Original Edition are still current and relevant.

Nevertheless, I decided that sooner was better than later in this case, since a few key developments have taken place in the online publishing world that I think warrant inclusion in this Revised Edition of *Instant Book Writing Kit*. That is, some resources recommended previously have disappeared and/or changed, while other new ones have become available in the last couple of years.

In addition, since I penned the 2004 version of this book I have created, published, and marketed an additional half dozen or so new and revised books and ebooks. So I am able to pass on any new lessons that I have learned in this Revised Edition.

Unlike the "revised editions" of some books, this is more than just a quick update of the original material. Care was taken to reread every page and update and test all links to external websites. In fact, a full 20 pages of new content has been added.

PURPOSE OF THIS BOOK

The primary purpose of this book is to show anyone who wants to know -- and who is willing to purchase this book -- the exact process that I use to write, publish, and market my books and ebooks, both online and offline.

Although, the emphasis here will be mostly online since, as far as I'm concerned, that's the only way to do it these days. I'll explain the reasons why a little later on.

So, please regard this book/ebook as a step-by-step instruction manual that you can follow when developing your own books/ebooks.

I have come to call that process the Online Publishing Model.™

There's no single reason why I decided to write this book. As usual, it's a bit more complicated than that.

Here's a quick list of the main reasons why I wrote this book:

- Having written, published, and marketed more than a dozen books/ebooks for online distribution in the last few years, I feel that I am knowledgeable and experienced enough to pass on that knowledge and experience to others with some level of authority and credibility.

- I feel compelled to share my complete disillusionment with the traditional book publishing model and industry so that others wouldn't have to naively learn about it the hard way, as I did.

- I wanted people to know that I have developed and documented a simple, straightforward step-by-step model for making a decent living through online e-publishing – a model of which very few people are aware.

- My research indicates that there is a definite gap in knowledge out there when it comes to telling authors exactly how to cross over from the traditional publishing model to the relatively new Online Publishing Model [TM].

- I am tired of seeing aspiring authors get sucked in by the "vanity publishers" on a daily basis, thinking that they have found "the answer". I want as many people as possible to realize through this book that there is a way to get their book "out there" without giving up control and needlessly spending a fortune.

- And last but not least, my research indicated that there is a healthy market of aspiring self-publishers out there looking for just this kind of information.

Granted, if you do the research you'll find a handful of websites and ebooks purporting to tell you all about how "you too" can write an ebook.

Many of these books/ebooks and/or websites will tell you that you'll be able to write and publish a wildly successful ebook in a matter of a few days (or even hours!), after which you're sure to make a lot of money.

Unfortunately, the books of this ilk that I have checked out are long on hype and short on "exactly" how to go about it. In reality, there IS a tad more involved in developing and marketing a book/ebook than they let on.

That's where the unique approach of this book comes in.

The overall purpose here is not so much to convince you how "you too" can write an ebook on your favorite topic, although there is an element of that.

Rather, I have written this book to focus more on the specific "how-to" aspect of the process, targeting people who already know that they have something they want to put between the covers of a book/ebook, but they don't quite know how to get there.

WHO THIS BOOK IS FOR

When I decided to write this book I had three main groups of people in mind.

The first group is made up of those small time authors like me who have been slaving away, trying to scratch out a living via the traditional publishing model, whether they've been using a commercial publisher or they've been self-publishing. I want to show those people that there is a much more efficient and profitable way to publish, distribute and sell their books than the model they've always had foisted on them by the conventional publishing industry.

The second group that I wrote this book for is comprised of those regular everyday people who have an idea that they would like to write a book or ebook but don't quite know how to go about it. I'm trying to head those people off at the pass, if you will, so that they get turned-on to the Online Publishing Model before stumbling blindly into the traditional model, just because they don't know any better.

Finally, **the third group** of people I would like to reach with this book is comprised of the hundreds of people that are already online for one reason or another but haven't yet had a chance to publish a book/ebook. Many of these people see it being done all around them but they just don't quite know how to go about it themselves. I believe that the information in this ebook will empower these people to finally do it for themselves.

For all three groups I wanted to demystify and clearly explain the workings of the Online Publishing Model so that they may embrace it as their own.

I hope I've achieved that, through this.

THIS IS NOT A SALES PITCH

Please understand that I am not trying to sell you anything here.

This is not some kind of typical Internet marketing pitch trying to get you to do it my way, or to buy additional products. I'm not trying to convince you of anything in particular. This is NOT an upsell to anything else.

In fact, you will notice that none of the links in this book that go to other Web sites and/or products are affiliate links.

You've bought the book. That's all I was looking for. Now I can tell you my story.

My sole purpose is to tell you, as clearly as I possibly can, exactly how I go about book/ebook publishing online, based on a model I have developed through unrelenting trial and error experience.

So you won't find the usual hype and smoke-and-mirrors copywriting techniques that one finds in the vast majority of Internet-related Web sites, books and ebooks.

I'm simply going to walk you through the specific process that I have developed and fine-tuned over the past two plus years to create, publish and market my own books/ebooks. Regard it as a "transfer of specific knowledge" from me to you.

By buying this book/ebook you have purchased personal access to this specialized and unique information that only I can give you on this particular subject.

And, as owner of this book, the information contained herein is now yours to use as you wish in your own online publishing efforts.

So, happy e-publishing!

TERMINOLOGY NOTES

To avoid confusion and to be consistent I have used standardized terminology throughout this book. Here's how I define them:

ebook

An electronic or digital document that appears to the eye to be <u>exactly</u> the same in format as a standard book when printed on paper or displayed online, <u>except that,</u> it's original form is an electronic file that must first be read by a special software reader, such as Adobe Reader, or equivalent.

book/ebook

These terms are used interchangeably throughout this document and mean one and/or the other, or both, depending on the context.

e-document

Any digital document created to be electronically downloaded from a website, or transferred by electronic means such as e-mail.

e-publishing

Any type of online electronic publishing activity whereby the e-document created is designed to be downloaded electronically or digitally from a website. Also known as digital publishing.

PDF

Adobe Corporation's portable document format (PDF) is the only format I consider relevant for an ebook. It is currently the de facto standard for e-documents online.

POD

Print-on-demand (POD) refers to the production of printed hard copy books and documents, one (or a few) at a time, whenever requested.

HOW I GOT FROM THERE TO HERE

For reasons of credibility I think it's important that I tell you a bit about my background and how I came to write a book/ebook about how-to write books/ebooks. If you're the typical person who buys this book you're likely to identify with my story on one or more levels.

I didn't start out expecting to become an author of books/ebooks.

But as John Lennon once wrote in one of his songs, "… life is what happens when you're busy making other plans".

LIFE <u>IS</u> WHAT HAPPENS…

In fact, if anyone had told me a few years ago that I would soon thereafter write and publish more than a dozen full-length books/ebooks and various editions thereof, over a five-year period, I would have told them, first of all, that they were crazy, and secondly, I would have said that such a feat is impossible for one person in any case.

But, as it turns out, I would have been wrong. Here's what happened…

Back in the late 1990s I suddenly found myself without a job. This came as a bit of a shock since I had just completed my MBA degree in 1996 and moved to Montreal to take a big management position with an international training agency.

It had looked like my future was all set. I seemed to be on the threshold of an international career path for the remaining 15 to 20 years of my working life.

Unfortunately, or perhaps fortunately as it turned out, in taking that new job I had jumped aboard a sinking ship. In fact, in a matter of 17 short and hectic months, my brief career with that international training agency had ended. Not long after, that organization disappeared into the sunset.

STARTING OVER ISN'T ALWAYS EASY

Finding myself unemployed for the first time in my adult life, my initial reaction was to launch into panic mode and immediately start searching for another regular position, or "job-job" as I now call those conventional types of jobs. After all, that's all I had really known up to that point.

I guess I forgot to mention that, by the time I earned my MBA via an executive MBA program in the mid 1990s, I had already worked in a variety of progressively more senior jobs during a 25-year career in government service.

So, aside from a bit of consulting work that I had done on the side, the government "big brother" scenario was about all I knew at the time, employment-wise.

Needless to say, after that period I was intimately familiar with "bureaucratic bafflegab" and the many other spirit-extinguishing downsides of working in a bloated bureaucracy where process invariably triumphs over substance.

Fortunately for me, before I jumped into serious job-hunting mode, I came to my senses and realized that more than 25 years of living from paycheck to paycheck and achieving very little in a lasting sense, was more than enough.

And, I reasoned that working for a large company wouldn't be much different from the government scenario. It's just a function of size more than anything else. I could see that I'd just be another one of thousands of "cubby-hole dwellers" waiting for retirement to eventually arrive. I cringe now, just thinking about such a fate.

It's not that I hadn't thought about leaving before. In fact, during my years as a civil servant I frequently fantasized about exiting the bureaucracy and doing something meaningful for myself.

A few times I even got close to escaping, but fear and life circumstances always conspired against me. I invariably chose the "easier, softer way". After all, there's nothing much more secure than a government paycheck coming in every two weeks, automatically, like clockwork, for a lifetime.

As it turned out, I didn't have to make the decision to leave for myself. A board of directors made it for me when it decided to eliminate my job (and others) at that international training institute in late 1997.

I knew in my "heart of hearts" that it was definitely time for me to move on to other more creative challenges in my life, beyond a 9 to 5 job-job with "big brother". It was this one certainty that sustained and motivated me through that difficult period.

ON MY OWN AT LAST

So, in early 1998 I hung out my shingle as a private consultant, business writer, and publisher.

Sounds easy enough, but it wasn't. Like everyone else I had to pay my dues and learn a lot of things the hard way. Fact is, I've always been an "experiential" learner.

It took me about two years to become completely disillusioned with business consulting and professional copy writing. In fact I was shocked to find out the many negative aspects of what I had always seen from the outside as "freedom":

- I soon realized that there were only so many hours in a day that I could be working as a consultant/writer, thus limiting me to a fixed income, just like when I worked for the government -- except there were no fringe benefits.

- My former government "bosses" had simply been replaced by demanding and frequently ungrateful "clients". At least bosses had a direct interest in keeping me happy as an employee by providing decent pay and working conditions. Clients had no stake whatsoever in the success or well-being of me or my business.

- I was frequently nickeled and dimed by clients. Many clients "used" their option to switch to a competitor as leverage to squeeze me down to the lowest possible per diem rate, meaning that I often had to work for fees much lower than what I was worth as a professional.

- The only time I ever received feedback from clients was when they wanted more, or when there was a problem. No matter how hard I might have worked to produce a high quality product that I was proud of, it was rare to receive any kind of positive feedback from a client. Their attitude always seemed to be, "after all we paid for it."

- Each time you get a new client you have to prove yourself all over again from scratch. Since the new client does not know you, and you haven't worked with them before, one often has to spend a lot of time and effort showing them that you are indeed qualified for the job.

As you can see from the above, life as an independent consultant isn't necessarily all it's cracked up to be. So, I pursued other options in parallel with consulting.

MY FIRST BOOK

One thing led to another, and by the end of 1999 I had written and self-published my first standard paperback book, *"Internet Basics without fear! Quick-Start Guide For Becoming Internet-Friendly In Just A Few Easy Steps"*.

That book was my very first venture into the world of conventional book publishing. It was a self-help/how-to book aimed at people who were missing out on the benefits of the Internet due to their fear of technology. (Early days of the Net).

But, I didn't just say one day "I think I'll write a book", and then start writing the following day. The idea evolved over a number of months and was partly influenced by watching what my own father had gone through while becoming familiar with the Internet.

In late 2000 I self-published the *Revised Edition* of that book, once again using the traditional book publishing model.

Overall, the two editions of *Internet Basics* didn't do too badly, and I did manage to sell over 4,500 of them in total. Not too bad for my first self-publishing effort on a marketing budget of close to zero.

But I certainly didn't get rich either, especially considering that I was using the conventional book publishing model. It paid my direct expenses, but that's about all.

Nevertheless, that learning experience with the traditional book publishing model later proved invaluable when I started looking into the possibility of going "online" and publishing my work in electronic form as ebooks.

Indeed, it was my initial experiences with the traditional book publishing model that soon convinced me that e-publishing is the only way to go these days.

Later on in this book I'll give you some details as to exactly why the traditional book publishing model is highly dysfunctional from a business perspective, and why the only way to go these days is with the e-publishing of ebooks online; and ideally, a combination of ebooks and "print-on-demand" (POD) books.

For now, I'll just say that my original experiences with the traditional book publishing industry were less than rewarding. In fact, they were a rude awakening.

It didn't take me long to realize that there was no way that I could make a decent living as a self-published author going the conventional route.

So as I was saying, by late 2000 I was without a job-job, had failed using the traditional book publishing model, and had concluded that independent consulting was a dog-eat-dog dead-end.

GOING ONLINE

Things weren't looking too promising as I rang in the New Year on January 1, 2001, to say the least. People close to me were starting to subtly suggest that maybe I just wasn't meant to be doing my own thing; that perhaps I should be looking for conventional employment again.

I knew in my heart and my wallet that time was running short and it wouldn't be long before I would have to admit total defeat and re-enter the world of bureaucracy once again. Ugghhh!

But I also knew there was one last faint hope for me… an Internet-based business.

During my online travels as a consultant and writer it had quickly become clear to me that a certain group of individuals, some of them in situations similar to mine, were actually making their living online. In fact, it appeared that a few of these online entrepreneurs were doing very well.

Seeing this, I just knew I had to give myself one last shot at doing it on my own.

Desperate, I borrowed enough money to keep me afloat for a couple more months, signed up for every line of credit for which I still qualified, and started studying everything I could get my hands on that would show me how to make money online via the Internet.

I won't bore you with the details of that process right now, except to say that over a six-month period I threw myself into all-consuming total immersion learning mode, absorbing as much as I possibly could about how to make a living online. (Besides, the details of that story might be the basis for another book!).

FINDING MY ONLINE GURU

Early on in my quest for online income, I stumbled across a certain "Internet marketing guru", as they are called in the online world. I won't mention his name here because that's not the point. Suffice it to say that he had been online for a few years by then, and had already experienced a couple of major successes.

The point is that this guru-guy convinced me that all I had to do to make a modest living online was to take three simple steps as follows:

- create a theme-oriented, quality-content, free-information website to which targeted visitors would flock from the search engines;

- fill that website with in-context affiliate links going to the websites of merchants selling products related to the theme of my free-information site;

and then presto…

- affiliate commissions would start rolling in as the visitors that were referred from my site bought products at those merchant websites.

It's called "affiliate marketing". I just wish it was as easy as guru-guy had said.

It's great in theory folks, but I'm here to tell you otherwise. Unless you get very lucky and happen to stumble across the right combination of high-priced products that sell well, are directly related to your main area of interest, and, the merchants pay unusually high commissions -- your chances of making a living online exclusively as an "affiliate marketer" are very slim.

There is in fact, a very small group of people who are successfully making their entire living from affiliate commissions. These people are known as "super affiliates" and they are a rare breed indeed.

I'll tell you about one of those successful super affiliates who I am quite familiar with as an online friend and colleague. Her name is Rosalind Gardner, and she is one of the elite few who have beaten the odds. I'll tell you more about Rosalind in the Joint Venture part of Market Your Book/eBook (See page 117).

In most cases, super-affiliates are successful due to a combination of right-time/right-place and good luck, coupled with links to high price/margin products which are directly related to their particular specialized information niche.

In fact, I would like to challenge any one of these established "super affiliates" to apply their exact same methods and techniques to other niches, and see how successful they would be in those. Say for example, my "writing help" niche.

You can trust me on this one folks, it wouldn't happen. There definitely will never be any "writing help related" super affiliates.

So, if anyone tries to sell you the "affiliate marketing model" as your one-and-only ticket to online riches, get out your salt shaker real quick.

CHOOSING THE RIGHT PATH

Now, where was I before going off on my little affiliate marketing tangent?

Oh yes, I was explaining how I spent my first six months online learning everything I could about how some people manage to make their entire living online. In one sentence, here's the bottom-line on how-to make one's living online…

You MUST create your very own products and/or services and sell them from your own website(s).

Believe me, this is the only sure way for the average person to make a decent steady income online.

Even the so-called gurus who promote various ways to make money online, concede when pressed that the most surefire way for you to make a significant steady income online is through developing and selling your own products and/or services.

So, if you are a writer or someone thinking about writing a book or ebook, this is very good news indeed!

And here's some more good news… even if you don't regard yourself as a writer you can still write a book/ebook – really! As long as you know how to talk, and are capable of writing that down you won't have a problem producing a book/ebook on any subject on which you are knowledgeable.

This is also very good news, because it just so happens that the single best way to make money online from your own product is by selling your own ebook.

That's exactly why I've written this ebook to tell you everything you need to know and do to write, publish and market your own book and/or ebook online!

YES, I DID WRITE A DOZEN HOW-TO BOOKS

Who would have ever guessed that during the 27 months from July 2001 to October 2003, I would be able to single-handedly write, publish and market a total of 7 books/ebooks online? Not me. Believe me, that was an intense period!

I slowed down a bit after that, but even then, I did manage to write three more new books as well as do major revisions to five of my earlier books/ebooks. So, if you count everything -- new books plus major revisions to previously published books – the total comes to about 15 books/ebooks published over a half-dozen years.

Here I am surrounded by some of my titles once they were published in paperback form using print-on-demand (POD) technology. The first version of each of these books was an ebook, all of which continue to be sold and downloaded every day from my network of websites.

As I stated earlier, up until a few years ago I knew precious little about this whole subject of e-publishing. In fact, I didn't have a clue what this mysterious term "ebook" even meant.

EBOOKS DEMYSTIFIED

When I first got online, the people there were throwing the ebook word around left, right, and center. But it was hard to get a good fix on exactly what these ebooks were all about, and how they worked.

The whole thing sounded very "techie" to me, so I initially dismissed ebooks as something for the techno-nerds, but not for us regular people.

But, it just wouldn't go away. More and more of the gurus were touting ebooks as the next big wave online. Savvy Internet marketing experts were calling ebooks the key to online success and income.

You'd pick up the newspaper and some publishing expert or another would be waxing eloquent about how ebooks and e-publishing were soon to be the future of the international publishing business.

I couldn't ignore it any longer. I had to get to the bottom of this ebook thing. So, I purchased and downloaded a few Internet marketing "how-to" ebooks just to see what these mysterious things were all about.

Lo and behold, I discovered that ebooks were just like regular books, except that you downloaded them onto your computer hard drive and then used special "free", easy-to-install software to read them. I also found out that you could even print them out and have a hard copy, just like with a standard book!

For me, realizing what an ebook actually was, became an instant "eureka" experience!

Having recently gone through my less-than-rewarding experiences with the standard book publishing model, I could immediately see the possibilities of ebooks from the independent writer/publisher's perspective .

So, in the summer of 2001 I sat down to write my very first ebook. The one that you're reading right now is the Revised Edition of number eight, which was initially published in 2004.

MY BOOKS/EBOOKS TO-DATE

The following is a list of the full-length books/ebooks that are currently available online which I wrote and published between July 2001 and March 2008:

Instant Home Writing Kit (Revised Edition)
How To Save Money, Time and Effort and Simplify Everyday Writing Tasks
http://instanthomewritingkit.com

Instant Business Letter Kit (Revised Edition)
How To Write Business Letters That Get The Job Done
http://instantbusinessletterkit.com

Instant Recommendation Letter Kit (Third Edition)
How To Write Winning Letters of Recommendation
http://instantrecommendationletterkit.com

Instant Reference Letter Kit -
How To Write Powerful Letters of Reference
http://instantreferenceletterkit.com

Instant Resignation Letter Kit -
How To Write A Super Resignation Letter and Move On With Class
http://instantresignationletterkit.com

Instant College Admission Essay Kit (Revised Edition)
How To Write A Personal Statement Essay That Will Get You In
http://instantcollegeadmissionessay.com

Instant Letter Writing Kit -
How To Write Every Kind of Letter Like A Pro
http://instantletterwritingkit.com

Writing Success Secrets (Revised Edition)
Practical Tips and Tricks For Everyday Writing
http://writinghelptools.com/secrets.html

Instant Book Writing Kit (Revised Edition)
How To Write, Publish and Market Your Own Money-Making Book (or eBook) Online
http://instantbookwritingkit.com

How To Write A "How-To" Book (or eBook)
Make Money Writing About Your Favorite Hobby, Interest or Activity
http://howtowritehowto.com

Internet Basics for Beginners
How To Send E-Mails and Surf the Net With Ease
http://writinghelptools.com/ibasics/ibmainpage.html

Whew, I'm glad I made it through that! I got tired just listing them there!

These are just the currently available versions of those publications. As I mentioned earlier, I have produced Revised Editions to half a dozen of the above, including a Third Edition to my best selling *Instant Recommendation Letter Kit*.

My eBooks are unique in the sense that they provide comprehensive "how-to" information <u>combined with</u> "real-life" templates that users can download into their word processors and use as they choose.

The books range in length from 110 pages and 25,000 words to 260 pages and 80,000 words. As you can tell by their length, these are not little information booklets. They are actual full-length books, packed full of useful content directly relevant to the needs of their readers.

At the following link you will find a brief summary of what each ebook is about:
http://writinghelptools.com

LEARNING THROUGH EXPERIENCE

Almost all of my books/ebooks to-date have been directly related to my particular online niche -- English language "writing help" for the day-to-day practical writing needs of the average person. They are designed to meet the home, business, and educational writing needs of the typical visitor to my writing help websites.

My free content "writing help" website is actually my "research lab" when I'm wondering about what writing-related product to develop next. I carefully study the behavior of visitors to the pages of that site and that gives me a pretty fair idea of the type of writing-related information that people are looking for. Here's that site:
http://writinghelp-central.com

Naturally, while writing, publishing, and marketing my books/ebooks during the past few years I have learned a lot of things -- some of them the hard way. Through that process I've found out what works best, what doesn't work as well, and what just doesn't work at all. Along the way I've also found a number of shortcuts which have allowed me to streamline the process.

As a result of those experiences I would say that I could easily develop a quality 100+ page ebook from the simple concept stage through to the point where it is available for sale download on a website, in a matter about of 4 weeks.

Let's say 25 to 30 days for everything, starting from a blank page or screen.

By following the step-by-step information I give you in this book, you should also be able to create your own ebook from scratch within roughly the same time-frame.

TRADITIONAL PUBLISHING – A BROKEN MODEL

As I've already stated a number of times, this ebook is all about NOT using the traditional book publishing model.

As far as I'm concerned the traditional model is so fraught with problems I am amazed that it even works at all for a few people.

Some readers may be quite familiar with the characteristics of the conventional model, so if you're one of those please bear with me through this short section of the book. I think it's important to itemize exactly what I'm talking about before I dump all over it.

Please take note that everything I state in this section is from the perspective of an individual author who is about to write a book and wants to get it published and marketed. That's somewhere close to where you're at right now, I trust.

If you are an author, the traditional model normally involves two basic choices: 1) use a commercial publisher, or 2) self-publish.

THE COMMERCIAL PUBLISHER ROUTE

This option involves the author submitting book proposals or full manuscripts to commercial publishing houses in the hope of acceptance. In some cases the author will have to hire an agent to represent him/her to the publishing houses.

Once a manuscript is accepted by a publishing house (the vast majority submitted are not accepted) a contract is signed between the author and the publishing house.

This will kick-off a time consuming and often complex process involving printers, shippers, wholesalers, distributors, marketers, and finally, booksellers.

All of these activities are managed on the author's behalf by the publishing house and/or its agents or sub-contractors.

With this model it can take a long time for things to happen. In a typical case it could take anywhere from 18 to 24 months from the time the author finishes a book manuscript, until the actual book gets to the bookshelves.

THE SELF-PUBLISHING ROUTE

The self-publishing option is where the author eliminates some of the middlemen and manages the overall publishing, distribution and marketing processes him/herself.

Consequently, the author has much more personal control of the whole process and can earn more money per copy than if going through a publisher. This option involves a lot of work by the self-publisher who has to either perform, or arrange for all of the functions and services that a publisher would normally look after.

This model is normally less time-consuming in terms of elapsed time, since there is no manuscript submission and approval process involved. Other than that, the book that is printed though the self-publisher is subject to the same publishing cycle as with a regular publisher. On average, the self-publishing process could save 6 to 12 months over the conventional publisher model.

For the two editions of my original *Internet Basics* paperback I used the self-publishing model for three main reasons: less time to get my book to the shelves, more control over the process, and make more money on each sale.

This approach worked to the extent that my books did reach the shelves within two months of being printed, and I did make more money on each sale.

However, I learned there were numerous downsides to the traditional model.

TWO TYPICAL HORROR STORIES

As I went through the entire self-publishing process twice, I did encounter various problems. Following are very brief descriptions of two typical situations that I experienced as a self-publisher, just to give you a flavor for the kinds of problems that one can run into using the standard book publishing model:

1. My supposedly respectable American book distributor went bankrupt (management fraud actually) and I never saw a penny for the 750 books that I had shipped to them. They sold over 500 copies and then kept the money. This kind of experience is not uncommon in the book publishing industry.

2. My Canadian distribution and order fulfillment company closed down because its parent publishing company declared bankruptcy. As a result, I could not gain access to my books for many weeks and I finally had to pay a fee to have them shipped to the warehouse of another distributor for storage.

Both of the above situations also involved hundreds of other small-time self-publishers just like me. These are just anecdotal illustrations of the kind of things that can happen. I won't even go into the dozens of administrative and financial problems that occurred on an ongoing basis.

Honestly, based on my first-hand experience with the North American book publishing and distribution industry, in my opinion, it has to be one of the most archaic and poorly run business models that I have ever encountered. The entire industry seems to be decades behind the typical current-day business models of most other industries. It's shocking really.

Trust me. If there's any way that you can possibly side-step the conventional book publishing model, do so.

The good news is that I'm going to tell you exactly how to do that in this ebook.

THE SHOCKING DOWNSIDES

In order to make sure you get my point, and understand exactly how backward, outdated and dysfunctional the entire conventional book publishing industry business model is, I'm going to give you a few specifics below.

Here's what the conventional book publishing industry offers you...

Give Away Half Your Book's Value Up-Front

If your book's cover price is, say $30, you will have to discount at least 40% to 60% right off the top when selling your book to wholesalers and retailers. So, from the very outset you will be working from an actual price of somewhere between $12 and $18. That means that any portion of the eventual sale you get will be based on the $12 to $18, not the $30.

Don't Count On Making Much Money

If you choose the commercial publisher option the best you can hope to receive for your book is a royalty somewhere between 6% and 10% of the "net". The "net" is the amount the publisher receives, <u>after</u> discounting to retailers. Example; cover price = $30; discount to large retail chain = $15 (i.e. 50%). Your cut would be somewhere between $0.90 and $1.50 per book sale. Really.

So, for selling 5,000 copies (which is a very good sales figure) you would receive a grand total of somewhere between $4,500 and $7,500. At that rate you'll have to write 12 or more books per year just to gross an annual income over $60K!

Plan To Write Lots Of Books

If you choose the self-publishing option, your main distributor will give you somewhere around 55% of the of the cover price of your book. Using our $30 cover price example, that works out to $16.50 per sale that goes to you under this scenario. However, certain unavoidable production and overhead expenses need to be deducted from that amount. For example, the cost of printing your book, say $4 per book in this example. You will also be responsible for advertising, marketing and publicity costs, not to mention the cost of shipping books to buyers and distributor(s).

Let's say those other costs total another $4 per book. So, for 5,000 books sold you would net 5,000 x ($16.50-$8.00 = $8.50) = $42,500. From this you need to deduct a certain amount for office expenses and other business expenses as well. You might only have to write and self-publish two to three books per year to gross over $60K annually under this 5,000 book sales scenario. But don't forget, this option requires your ongoing personal time and effort involvement.

Wait Forever To Get Paid

Typically, you will have to wait between 90 days and 120 days after an actual book sale before you will receive your payment for that sale. I still shake my head at this one. How does the publishing industry get away with such an archaic practice in the 21st Century? In normal business the standard wait for payment is usually 30 days, sometimes as much as 60 days; but 90 to 120 days to pay a poor struggling author? It's a crying shame that they still manage to get away with it.

I tell you folks, this is no way to treat people, but as long as the publishing industry gets away with it, this practice won't change. This kind of payment delay is the norm, whether you go through a commercial publisher or if you're a self-publisher.

Issue 100% Refunds On Unsold Books

A trademark feature of the conventional book publishing industry is the way in which it deals with "returns". In almost all cases -- publishers, distributors, wholesalers and retailers – they maintain the right to return unsold books to you, the author, for a 100% refund, even many months later. Let's say you sell 200 copies of your book to a particular retail chain through your publisher (commercial publisher model) or through your distributor (self-publisher model).

First, you will have to wait 90 to 120 days to get paid for those 200 sales. Then, let's say that after five months, various stores in the retail chain find that 45 unsold copies of your book are still on their shelves. The company would then send those books back to your publisher or distributor for a 100% refund. Your publisher or distributor then immediately deducts these 100% refunds from your account! That's right.

I'm not kidding people, this is how it works! There is absolutely no incentive for bookstores or publishers/distributors to make any effort whatsoever to move your book off their shelves since they know you will provide a 100% rebate for all their "returns" in any case. I still have trouble getting my mind around this one!

Give Them Extra Money, Just In Case

As soon as you start getting paid for your first sales, 90 to 120 days late of course, you will NOT receive the full amount to which you are entitled. Instead, your publisher or distributor will withhold 25% or more from your payment right up-front to cover the possibility of eventual returns of unsold and/or damaged books months down the line. In other words, they deduct anticipated returns in advance.

So, not only do they hold 100% of your money hostage for at least three to four months, they then add insult to injury by withholding another 25% or more of your money well into the future as a contingency. And, don't even think about getting an interest adjustment for the money they withhold. It won't happen.

Get Stuck In Someone Else's Time Cycle

Most commercial publishers operate on a time-frame of 18 months from approved/accepted manuscript until the book is released for sale. If you are a self-publisher you can whittle this down to maybe 3 to 6 months depending on when your book is ready vis a vis your distributor's catalog publication schedule. As a self-publisher, if you time it perfectly or just get lucky there might only be 6 to 8 weeks between your book being ready to ship and it getting onto store shelves.

A typical example of this was the distribution for my first *Internet Basics* book. Each year my distributor issued four catalogues, one for each season. These catalogues are sent out to the book buying industry four times a year on a very fixed schedule. Before your book will be ordered by the book buyers you have to prepare your catalog listing and ensure that you get it into the distributor's catalog in time, or you'll have to wait for the following catalog three months later.

I trust that the foregoing points have made my case against the conventional book publishing and distribution industry absolutely clear. From an author's and/or self-publisher's perspective it is a highly dysfunctional, badly flawed business model that wouldn't survive in most industries.

In fact, the system is so stacked against the average author I'm amazed that some people actually try to eke out an ongoing living in that thankless industry.

I guess those people feel they have no other choice, or they are hoping against the odds that one day they will pen a mega best-seller. Good luck! For similar odds, it would involve a lot less effort to go out and buy a lottery ticket.

So, here's my bottom line on the conventional book publishing and distribution business...

If you are an author or aspiring author, and you're hoping to make a modest living writing and publishing your own books or ebooks, the traditional book publishing and distribution model is definitely NOT the way to go.

Don't waste your time and effort. Don't even think about it.

Now for the good news…

The good news is that over the past few years a new publishing model has evolved that eliminates all of the negative aspects of the traditional publishing model and adds a number of benefits.

I call it the "Online Publishing Model™".

The remainder of this ebook is going to tell you exactly what that the Online Publishing Model is all about and how you can harness it to publish and then market your own book/ebook through multiple channels.

ONLINE PUBLISHING – THE NEW MODEL

As I already stated, I have been personally exploring the intricacies of the Online Publishing Model™ (OPM) since late 2001. Since then, I have written, published, marketed and sold more than a dozen books/ebooks through various online channels.

ONLINE DISTRIBUTION CHANNELS

Once your book/ebook is written, there are a number of online channels through which you can distribute and sell your book/ebook, as follows:

Dedicated Sales-Mini-Site

First and foremost, once your book/ebook is written you need to create what's called a "mini website" (i.e. sales-mini-site) for the sole purpose of selling that product. Trust me, this is the only way to go. You MUST have a site dedicated to the sale of that one book/ebook. Search engines will send targeted traffic to your site and your site sales/info copy will make the sale online.

Digital Download Distributors

These are digital fulfillment companies that distribute downloadable ebooks to the largest online bookstores such as amazon.com, barnesandnoble.com, and many other sellers of ebooks. These companies are happy to put your ebook in front of thousands of traditional book buyers who normally wouldn't see it. Listing your digital download ebook with one of these distributors is essential.

Print-On-Demand Distributors

These are distributors that use a relatively new technology called print-on-demand (or POD). You provide the company with a digital copy of your book, plus some cover artwork in digital form, and they will set up your book so that single book orders can be printed and drop-shipped directly to the buyer. This allows you to provide a hard copy version (of your ebook) to those customers who insist on it, while you only pay the cost of printing a single copy. (No more printing 2,000+ copies up-front just to get a reasonable cost per copy!).

Other Distribution Channels

There are a few other distribution channels as well, such as small online ebook stores, but these are relatively minor, and to-date I just don't think they're worth the trouble. The important thing is to focus online on driving targeted visitors to your sales-mini-sites.

Suffice it to say, there are at least three highly effective channels by which you can distribute and sell your book/ebook online through the Online Publishing Model™.

I will give you more details on these distribution channels later on when I get into the "how-to" portion of this book.

BENEFITS OF THE ONLINE MODEL

I realize that the previous section describing all of the negative aspects of the traditional book publishing model might have been a bit depressing, but take heart, everything in this section is good news for anyone wanting to publish a book/ebook.

The benefits of the Online Publishing Model™ are numerous and compelling:

You'll Pocket More Money

With the online publishing model you'll be able to net anywhere from 3 to 30 times more per book than what you would under the conventional model. For example, when I sell an ebook from one of my websites today for US $30 I get to keep about $27 of that. Compare that with a net of between $0.90 and $8.50 under the traditional model. (See page 26). The only middleman involved in the online model is the company I use to securely process the credit card payment, called a payment processor. Even when using an online distribution company as a middleman, you'll makes a lot more from each sale that with the traditional model.

You Can Charge Higher Prices

When you offer your book/ebook through the online publishing model, people will be willing to pay more just to be able to get the information immediately. Generally speaking, people will pay higher prices online than they normally would for the same thing offline due to the "instant gratification factor". This will be especially the case if your ebook offers them the instant information they are looking for packaged and/or organized in a unique way that they can't find elsewhere.

This applies more to non-fiction information products and "how-to" books/ebooks than it does to fiction books. Although I'm sure if one really puts their mind to it they could find ways to add a downloadable component(s) to a fiction ebook that would entice people to purchase and download it online for a premium price.

You'll Get Paid Sooner

With the online publishing model you'll definitely get your money faster. For ebook sales made from my websites I receive checks in the mail two weeks after the sales period closes, making it on average, about three weeks from the sale date until I get paid. For sales through my online distributor there's a 90-day delay, similar to the traditional model. However, the checks are bigger and therefore more worth waiting for, and there are no holdbacks to cover possible "returns". (See page 28).

Your Costs Will Be Way Lower

Naturally, with the online publishing model there will be no printing costs for the digital download version of your ebook. Even when you factor in the costs of hosting a website (about $60 per year) and the one-time cost of having someone else create your sales mini-site for you (say, $500 to $1000), these costs are way lower than out-of-pocket costs under the traditional model.

With the traditional publishing model, in order to keep your per-unit costs down, and to benefit from economies-of-scale, you need to get your book printed in large quantities. Typically you'll need to print a minimum of 1,000 copies to get a reasonable per unit cost. So, for a typical 150 page paperback book this means you will have an initial cash outlay for printing of anywhere from $2,000 to $4,000, depending on the detailed specifications of the job and the pricing structure used.

For the print-on-demand version of your book you will pay for printing on a per-copy basis ONLY. For example, for each POD version of my book *Internet Basics For Beginners*, I pay $4.34, for a single <u>already-sold</u> book.

Returns Are A Non-Issue

If you produce a quality ebook that your visitors are looking for and you sell it from your Web site as a downloadable product, you will have very few refund requests. My refund rate (i.e. returns) at all of my websites is less than 1%. For digital downloads, and print-on-demand books sold on your behalf by companies such as amazon.com, refunds are simply not applicable. (See page 28).

You'll Be In Control

As an online author/publisher you will control almost every aspect of the publication and marketing process for your book/ebook. Using a sales-mini-site you will have almost complete control of every aspect of your sales and distribution process. Whenever you like, you can change the price, the sales copy, the payment processor – you can change whatever you want, whenever you want. If you're using an online distributor/publisher you will still have much more flexibility and control than with distributors/publishers under the traditional model.

You Can Publish At Will

Using the online publishing model you can publish your new ebook whenever you like. Just upload it to your website whenever you're ready. Same thing when you use an online distributor. Just send them your new ebook or POD file whenever you have it ready. They'll have it up on their websites within a week or so.

Under the conventional publishing model you are automatically locked into the rigid annual time cycle of that industry. You don't have a choice. To get your book publicized properly you need to meet a number of fixed deadlines of that industry so that your book can be listed in various catalogues and directories. You have no control over this. Miss those deadlines, and your book will be delayed for another few months. (See page 29).

No Inventory To Manage

There will be no inventory to manage or track with the online publishing model. Naturally, since you won't have any physical books to produce, you won't have to worry about shipping hundreds or thousands of copies to your publisher/distributor and there will be no inventory for you to keep track of. What's more, there will be no returns due to books damaged while in transit, or in the distributor warehouses. Both of these are common occurrences under the traditional model, by the way.

Make Revisions Whenever You Like

With the online publishing model you can revise and start distributing the new version of your ebook/book whenever you're ready to. Whether you're selling your ebook through your own website, or as a digital download and/or POD through a distributor/publisher, you can make revisions whenever you like and just upload the latest version to wherever it's being sold from. No more worries about the publishing industry's catalog deadlines, etc. (See page 29).

You Can Include Unique Features

Since you have more flexibility and control with the online model you can add value added features and bonuses to your book/ebook as you wish.

For example, with all of my writing kit ebooks, not only do my buyers get a complete ebook in pdf format, but I also provide them with a downloadable MS-Word file containing all of the fully-formatted letter and other document templates from the main book that they can download into their word processors and work with. This is definitely a value-added feature that one wouldn't normally get with a standard book under the conventional model.

I even offer this same download option to people who buy my digital download book or POD book via amazon.com, barnesandnoble.com, etc., through my online distributor. In both of those documents I provide a Special Preface with a special e-mail address that owners may use to request that the templates be sent to them.

A couple of years ago I decided to offer my *Writing Success Secrets* ebook as a Special Bonus for people buying the writing kits offered at certain of my websites. This was easy to do with the online model. I simple added some new copy to the sales page advising prospects of the new bonus offer and I added an extra download link to each of my download pages so that buyers can get the new bonus when downloading the main ebook, without any special intervention by me.

Easy and Timely Access To Information

With the online publishing model you'll have close to real-time access to your sales information. Since everything with the online model happens via the Net, you'll have direct and timely access to your sales data 24/7.

For example, every single time I sell a product on one of my websites I receive an e-mail from my payment processor advising me of such. Any time I want to check on my overall sales situation I just sign-in to my account at my payment processor's Web site and I can access my financials immediately.

Even with my online distributor/publisher I can go to their website and find out my sales-to-date information up until midnight yesterday.

Anyone who has worked with traditional publishing houses and distributors knows that the best that many of them seem to be able to come up with is a set of statements once a month by snail mail that cover a one-month period that ended six-weeks before. So instead of close to real-time info, you get 6-week old data.

I might add that the companies I dealt with in the conventional industry were sending me reports by snail mail that looked like they were designed in the 1960s; another sign of how far behind the times that industry is.

In Summary

I trust that the benefits of the online publishing model listed above, coupled with the numerous downsides of the conventional publishing model covered in the previous section have made it abundantly clear why I am convinced that the Online Publishing Model^{TM} is the only book publishing option that makes sense the age of the Internet.

In fact, I firmly believe that if you are an independent author and/or publisher, the OPM is the only realistic solution if you hope to make a living at it.

17 ACTION STEPS FOR ONLINE PUBLISHING SUCCESS

Before we get started, please don't be intimidated by the number 17.

I could have been devious and grouped these into 7, or 9, or 11 steps, to make the process seem simpler and less intimidating. Instead, I decided to go with the bigger number because it breaks the process down logically into 17 "bite size" discrete sets of related actions or tasks.

Using the lower number might look simpler but it would actually be making the process more complicated and messy.

You'll see that some of the 17 Steps involve sending a single e-mail or a simply sign-up for a particular service. I have broken these out separately because they are key stand-alone actions, each one important enough to be highlighted on its own.

INITIAL ASSUMPTIONS

Before you launch into implementing the following book/ebook-creation steps I think it's important that you understand how I have arrived at this specific set of action steps to create and market your book/ebook.

That is, how and why have I arrived at these particular steps and resources? What was I thinking about? What was I assuming? In fact, many of the assumptions that follow are things I have assumed about you, and where you're at as you read this, and as you get ready to apply the information in this book.

Accordingly, the following is a list of the key underlying assumptions I have made when assembling this particular list of 17 ebook creation action steps.

You Want A Simple Solution

I have tried to keep the following action steps as simple and straightforward as possible. My goal here is to try to present the process just as I if I were explaining it to a good friend or a student so that they could easily duplicate exactly what I've done, in order to create and market their own ebooks.

Along those lines, as much as possible I've tried to limit the contents of each step to essential information only, without going off on distracting detours and/or into lengthy sidebars to try to impress you with my general level of knowledge.

So, for the sake of simplicity and clarity I'm going to limit the information to "need to know information" only. No "fluff" or "filler" in this book!

You Want Best Practices

As the old expression states "… there's more than one way to skin a cat". That's definitely true of the type of information covered in this book/ebook.

What I have included in the following action steps are information and recommendations on what I have personally found to be the "best practices" or "best solutions" to deal with the particular problem at hand at the time I needed that information when developing my books/ebooks.

I have not tried every possible solution in every case, so it's possible that there's a better way to achieve some of the tasks that follow. What I can say though, is that the solutions that I have arrived at in each case are the result of a certain amount of "due diligence" research, and that they have worked well for me.

If you know of a better and/or less expensive resource for any of the tasks listed below, by all means go ahead and use it.

You Want A Professional Product

I've downloaded a lot of ebooks over the past few years. Many I've purchased, and some were free downloads. Believe me, there's a wide range when it comes to depth and quality of content when it comes to ebooks.

A select few of the ebooks I've downloaded have been truly exceptional, while many others have been of questionable content and quality.

When developing all of my writing help ebooks I have tried hard to provide my readers with quality content presented in a professional manner. I like to think my success in that area explains why my refund request rate is so low.

All of the information given in the action steps that follow is based on the assumption that you too are interested in producing a high quality product with highly relevant content for your readers.

You Want A Step-By-Step Blueprint

I have organized the following *17 Action Steps* so that you can follow them one-by-one in numerical sequence. If you follow all 17 Steps as directed, at the end of the process you will have a book/ebook already selling online.

As I stated earlier, my point here has not been to cover all possible solutions. Rather, I have focused on giving you the simplest and most effective solutions of which I'm aware at each stage. I know that they work because they are what I use.

So, please follow all 17 of the following action steps in sequence and/or as otherwise directed, and you won't go wrong.

You Understand The Writing Process

One of my basic assumptions about you, because you purchased this book/ebook, is that you have an understanding of the basic creative writing process. In other words, I am assuming that you have already crossed over that psychological barrier that tells you that you can't write a book.

Indeed, Steps 6 through 10 of the *17 Action Steps* contained later on in this book assume that you are already mentally prepared to write your book/ebook; all you need at this point is some "how-to" advice and pointers on the mechanical process of writing, revising, and editing your book/ebook.

If that is not quite the case for you at this stage, and you are still in need of some more fundamental convincing and cajoling about how you too can author a book/ebook, I have the perfect solution for you, as follows.

It's a Five-Part Teleseminar series called *Awaken the Author Within*^{TM}. It was developed by two long time educators and ebook authoring specialists, Glenn Detziel and Paul Jackson. These two high energy teaching and ebook enthusiasts have coached scores of aspiring authors through the very basics of the ebook creation and authoring process.

So if you're looking for some additional help in getting into the right frame of mind to create your own book/ebook, I recommend that you participate in Glenn and Paul's *Awaken the Author Within*^{TM} teleseminar series. Here's the link to sign-up: http://AwakenTheAuthorWithin.com

While you're there, be sure to pick-up your free ebook, ***Secrets of eBook Authoring.***

Once you've completed that teleseminar you will be able to come back to this ebook and zoom through the *17 Action Steps* that are detailed later in this ebook.

You Know What You Are Writing About

I have written this book under the assumption that you have some idea as to what general subject you want to write your book/ebook about.

This book is all about how to do IT once you know what IT is. It's NOT about how to find out WHAT you want to write your book/ebook about. That's a whole different undertaking in itself.

In Step 1, on researching your online book/ebook, there are some suggestions and tools covered there that could help you find your niche from scratch, but that's not really the purpose of that section. Its purpose is to help you zero in on exactly what aspect/angle your book/ebook will focus on within your given niche, based on an analysis of the market related to your already selected niche.

If you're not yet quite sure what your niche is, there is help available. In fact, there are entire ebooks written on the subject of how to find one's niche online. Here's one by Michael J. Holland that comes highly recommended by some top Internet marketing gurus, although I haven't used it myself. It's called *Strike It Niche!* http://www.strikeitniche.com

Non-Fiction Beats Fiction

Generally speaking, non-fiction "how-to" type books, or informational/reference books, sell better, and at higher prices, than do fiction books/ebooks online.

This is largely because people are willing to pay a premium for information and/or tools that will help them solve an immediate problem.

Nevertheless, one is still likely to do better with fiction using the online publishing model, considering all of the downsides of the traditional model in contrast to all of the benefits of the online model.

PDF Is The Only Way To Go

For the first couple of years I was online there was an ongoing debate as to whether downloadable ebooks should be offered in PDF format or another one known as exe format. As far as I'm concerned that debate is over and pdf is it. In fact I see very few ebooks being offered in exe format these days.

It's not hard to understand why pdf won the day.

Number one, it's completely platform independent. This means that it doesn't matter whether your operating system is MS-Windows, Mac, or any other platform, the pdf document will still be readable.

Number two, the pdf document that gets created is an <u>exact</u> duplicate of the original document you produced no matter what software was used to create it.

Finally, a large percentage of computer users already have Adobe's free PDF Reader software installed on their computers. If they don't, the download/install is a simple process that even newbies seem to handle okay.

So, if you want to produce a professional quality ebook or digital download book, make sure you do it in PDF format. Accordingly, throughout this book I am assuming the use of PDF format in all cases.

The next page contains a discussion of the latest developments in ebook formats.

That's it for my assumptions. Let's get on with creating your book/ebook!

And, don't forget to have fun! Creating your own book/ebook can be exciting and lots of fun!

About "Other" eBook Formats

A number of developments have taken place since I published the first version of this book/ebook back in 2004. Below is a quick summary of what's been happening.

By far, the most significant events that have taken place in the ebook world over the past couple of years have occurred at amazon.com.

In July 2006 amazon.com suddenly stopped carrying PDF ebooks (Adobe Reader) on their websites. It turned out that amazon had purchased a company based in France called MobiPocket that had developed ebook creation and reading software that targeted personal handheld devices.

It seems that amazon had made a corporate decision that the future of ebooks was that they would be read primarily using handheld PDA devices and smartphones, and not so much on home PCs. These include such devices as Microsoft's Pocket PC Reader, the Palm Os Digital Media Reader, and the Blackberry.

So, for a period of about one year if you wanted your ebook listed at amazon.com you had to create an account at MobiPocket and convert your files into their format using their conversion software.

http://www.mobipocket.com

Then in the summer of 2007 amazon.com made a major announcement that shook the ebook world when it released its handheld Wireless Reading Device, the Kindle.

Since that time, if you want to sell your ebook via amazon.com you have been required to convert your ebook files via amazon's Digital Text Platform (DTP) which formats ebooks for reading exclusively in its Kindle device.

The Kindle is a hand-held book reader which displays a book page-by-page on what amazon.com calls "electronic paper" simulating the look-and-feel of real paper. It is small, lightweight, wireless, and has a high-resolution screen. For a full sales pitch explaining its many features go to the following link:

http://www.amazon.com/dp/B000FI73MA/ref=nav_kinw_dgtx

Of course, the big downside to amazon's Kindle is that it forces both publishers and ebook readers to use that company's proprietary technology. Oh, did I mention that as I write this the Kindle costs $399; and the books you order need to be available in the Kindle Store which stocks only titles that have been converted to DTP format?

Clearly, amazon.com has put all of its eggs in one basket with this Kindle strategy. It is not clear how successful they have been to-date, and it will likely take a couple of years to see to what extent ebook readers embrace the Kindle.

Bottom Line For Publishers

If you have the time and inclination I suggest you experiment with both MobiPocket and amazon's Kindle formats to see what happens. For example, once you have converted a book into their format and listed it with them, what sales do you make?

However, I wouldn't recommend abandoning PDF format anytime soon. It is still the de facto standard for ebooks worldwide, so existing ebook retailers will be sticking with PDF for the foreseeable future. Also, you will want to continue creating your downloadable ebooks in PDF so that the typical PC user can download them from your websites into the ubiquitous Adobe Reader software.

Remember, the entire amazon.com strategy surrounding the Kindle and their DTP format is that people will increasingly want to read ebooks on handheld devices. Is this realistic? I personally don't think so based on my experience with ebooks and ebook readers. I guess we will all just have to wait and see what shakes out.

THE 17 ACTION STEPS IN SUMMARY

The following flowchart summarizes the *17 Action Steps* for quick reference.

STEP 1	DO YOUR RESEARCH UP-FRONT

- Find out exactly what people are searching for in your niche.
- Find out what the competition is doing in your niche.

STEP 2	BRAINSTORM YOUR TITLE

- Make sure your most important keywords are in your title.
- Choose a final title at this stage to facilitate rest of process.

STEP 3	GET YOUR BOOK/EBOOK REGISTERED

- Register copyright if required in your country of residence.
- Obtain an ISBN number for your title.

STEP 4	REGISTER YOUR DOMAIN NAME

- Select and register your domain name based on your title.
- Choose a ".com" URL for your domain name if possible.

STEP 5	ORDER YOUR COVER

- Make sure you hire a professional cover designer.
- Visualize your own cover concept as input to designer.

STEP 6	DECIDE ON KEY PARAMETERS

- Find ways to ensure your book will be at least 100 pages.
- Make all formatting decisions and create a working template.

STEP 7	DEVELOP TABLE OF CONTENTS

- Create a detailed Table of Contents as your working outline.
- Table of Contents becomes the "blueprint" for your book.

STEP 8   DEVELOP DETAILED CONTENT POINTS

- Drill down to a level of detail below headings/sub-headings.
- Post this outline and use it as your visualize guide when writing.

STEP 9   WRITE YOUR BOOK/EBOOK

- Use the Table of Contents template from Steps 6 and 7.
- Using the template, fill-in-the-blanks one page at a time.

STEP 10   EDIT AND REVISE YOUR BOOK

- Do a light edit during the actual writing process.
- Get someone else to review it and then do your own final edit.

STEP 11   CREATE/PUBLISH YOUR EBOOK

- Convert your word processing document to PDF format.
- Ensure the PDF creation software you use does complete job.

STEP 12   CREATE YOUR SALES-MINI-SITE

- Get mini-site hosted and set-up payment processing account.
- Develop mini-site sales copy and upload to Web host site.

STEP 13   LAUNCH YOUR BOOK/EBOOK

- Request testimonials from niche experts and other webmasters.
- Post testimonials and make special introductory offers.

STEP 14   ANNOUNCE YOUR BOOK/EBOOK

- Get registered in free and pay-per-inclusion search engines.
- Develop and issue a news release through a distribution service.

STEP 15	MARKET YOUR BOOK/EBOOK

- Write articles – Do joint ventures – Use affiliate program referrals.
- Ezine advertising – Create free mini-course – Publish newsletter.
- Identify and implement various other proven marketing strategies.

STEP 16	TAKE YOUR EBOOK DIGITAL

- Select digital fulfillment distributor that will list your ebook.
- Reformat files for digital distribution and then transfer files.

STEP 17	GO POD WITH YOUR EBOOK

- Select digital fulfillment distributor that will list your POD book.
- Arrange for additional artwork required for POD book.
- Reformat files for POD delivery and then transfer files.

The above summary is included here for overall review and presentation purposes. From hereon in I will refer to the above as the *17 Action Steps*.

Each one of these Steps is broken down into specific sub-tasks with supporting information and resource references in the following sections of this chapter.

If you follow all 17 of these Steps in numerical order as presented here I can guarantee you that you will come out the other end of the process with your own money-making ebook available for sale through a number of channels:

- as a download on your Website;
- as a digital download ebook through ebook retailers;
- as a print-on-demand printed book through book retailers.

I know that this formula works from first-hand experience. It's exactly what I have used to write, publish and market more than a dozen ebooks/books.

STEP 1: DO YOUR RESEARCH UP-FRONT

Whatever the subject of your book/ebook, make sure you do adequate background and market research of your concept and/or niche at the very outset. **This is an important step. Don't skip it.**

Many people have gone off the rails early by skipping this initial stage of the process. They get what they consider to be "a really great idea" for a book/ebook; and then go charging off developing their product only to find out later that they have gone terribly wrong.

Just because something interests you and it seems "like" a really good idea doesn't mean it's going to sell well. You need to do some homework up-front to test and confirm all of your initial assumptions.

Find Out What They Are Searching For

Nowadays, thanks to the power of the Internet, it is much easier to do some basic market research than it ever was before.

Whatever niche you are considering, you need to do some basic demand and supply research. First, you'll want to know what people are searching for online related to your subject. So, to do this you need to find out the popular "keyword phrases" related to your subject.

Not sure what your popular keyword phrases are? That's ok, it's not hard to find out. To do this, I suggest you try one or more of the tools mentioned below.

For example, say you're thinking of writing a how-to book about "furniture making". Before going too far with your book you will want to find out roughly how many people are looking for information on that subject, and what specific type of information they are seeking.

There are a number of useful free keyword research tools available. One that I like is jointly offered by google.com and wordtracker.com. It's called nichebot.com: http://www.nichebotclassic.com

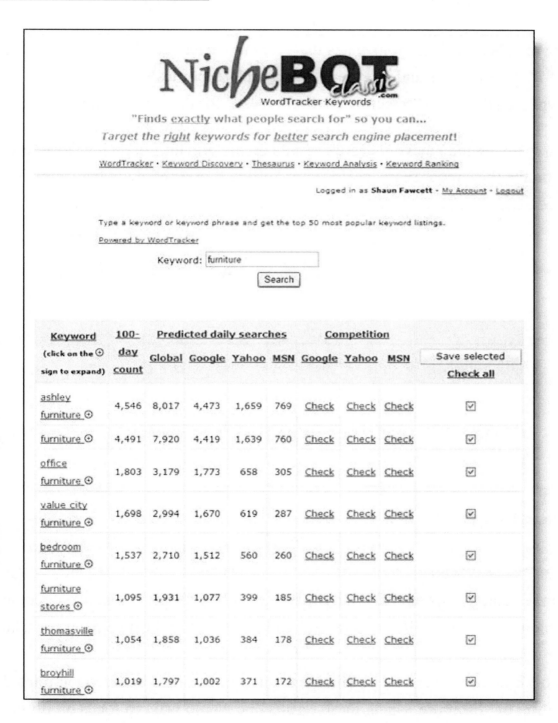

The above screen shot shows what NicheBot returned for a search on "furniture".

Nichebot results are powered by the search database maintained by a commercial keyword analysis service, wordtracker.com:

http://www.wordtracker.com

As I write this, Wordtracker.com states that "… our current database contains 316,558,816 search terms and represents the complete queries from the largest metacrawlers on the web (Metacrawler/Dogpile etc.) for the last 100 days."

For example, using the keyword search results on the previous page for "furniture", if I click on the third most-searched-for term "office furniture", I get the following:

Keyword (click on the ⊕ sign to expand)	100-day count	Predicted daily searches				Competition		
		Global	Google	Yahoo	MSN	Google	Yahoo	MSN
office furniture ⊕	1,803	3,179	1,773	658	305	Check	Check	Check
home office furniture ⊕	591	1,042	581	215	100	Check	Check	Check
used office furniture ⊕	222	391	218	80	37	Check	Check	Check
modern office furniture ⊕	192	338	188	69	32	Check	Check	Check
buy office furniture ⊕	141	248	138	51	23	Check	Check	Check
discount office furniture ⊕	129	227	126	46	21	Check	Check	Check
buying office furniture ⊕	120	211	117	43	20	Check	Check	Check
ergonomic office furniture ⊕	94	165	92	34	15	Check	Check	Check
modular office furniture ⊕	79	139	77	28	13	Check	Check	Check

Based on the "count" this tells me that the type of office furniture that most people are searching for is "home office furniture" followed by "used office furniture", etc.

Clearly, this kind of info can be invaluable to anyone writing a book/ebook related to the making of "furniture. Using these results one would want to focus on office furniture for the home office and perhaps include a chapter on the pros and cons of used furniture. These are illustrative examples of course.

Accordingly, you can go through the above search process for any keyword phrase that relates to your particular theme or niche.

What's great about NicheBot is that it not only tells you how many searches were made in the previous 100 days, but it also tells you how many daily searches are likely to be made for your keywords at the three major search engines: google.com, yahoo.com and msn.com. In addition, it provides direct links to the search results pages <u>for your keyword</u> at each of those search engines.

Nichebot is just one of about a dozen free keyword research tools that are available online. In addition, there are a number of powerful and sophisticated keyword research/analysis software programs that you can buy. For a comprehensive review and assessment of all of these tools you can check out Jay Stockwell's website at:
http://www.keywordworkshop.com/

A couple of years ago when I wanted to do some more sophisticated keyword research and analysis than was possible with the free tools, I purchased a software program called Keywords Analyzer that I have been very happy with.
http://www.keywordsanalyzer.com

Or, if you happen to have one of Ken Evoy's SBI! sites the keyword search and analysis tools are actually built right into the hosting package.
http://www.sitesell.com

Finally, if you're really serious about doing a comprehensive demand/supply analysis of your niche and proposed book/ebook, here's a more sophisticated tool:
http://www.productideaevaluator.com/

Benchmark The Competition

Once you have a handle on the main keyword phrases that people are searching for in your niche you'll want to take a detailed look at the top 30 or so results that come up for those phrases at some of the major search engines.

For this, go to a few key search engines, enter your main keyword search phrases at each one and see what comes up. As a minimum I suggest you use:

http://www.google.com

http://www.yahoo.com

http://www.msn.com

With these three you'll be covering well over 95% of all the pages on the Web. That should be enough to show you what's out there in terms of content related to your theme. Go to each one of those pages and see what kind of information is being offered in your niche, and how it is being delivered.

For example, when researching this particular book I went to the above search engines and sought out the titles of all books/ebooks I could find that have already been published online or offline on "write a book" or "write an ebook".

I also took a close look at all sites I could find that carried articles and other information related to the writing of ebooks.

Oh, one very important additional tool that will be essential to understanding your search engine results is the alexa.com toolbar. If you don't already have it installed on your browser do that right now. Here's the install page link:
http://download.alexa.com/index.cgi?p=Dest_W_b_40_T1

Over the past few years, alexa.com traffic rankings have become the accepted
standard among savvy webmasters for determining the relative importance of a site.
All you have to do is glance at the alexa.com ranking for a site and you will know
right away if you are dealing with a serious player that actually gets traffic and links.

Once you have the alexa toolbar installed it will give you valuable information about
each Web site you visit. Here's what the alexa.com install toolbar page looks like:

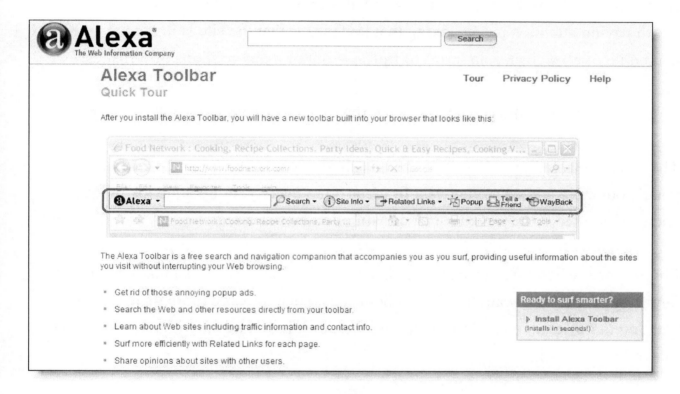

In the screen shot above, notice the "Site Info" label. Once you have that on your
own toolbar it will tell you the alexa.com "traffic ranking" for whatever site you
happen to be visiting. In addition, the toolbar has other useful features such as a pop-
up blocker, site link lists, and quick-click site contact links.

The following screen shot shows the toolbar of my browser with the Alexa toolbar
installed. It displays the alexa.com ranking for my Writing Help Central website as
72,713; placing it among the top 100,000 of all websites in terms of traffic.

This kind of information is invaluable of course because it gives you a good idea of the relative importance of a website in the big scheme of things online.

As a general rule of thumb, if a site has an alexa ranking of 500,000 or less, it is worth paying attention to. A ranking that low means that the site is in the top 1 percentile of all websites, in terms of traffic -- out of many millions of websites!

So pay attention to those websites with the low alexa.com ranking numbers.

The research techniques described above will give you a better handle on exactly what's out there and what you want to focus on to make your book/ebook unique and sought-after at the same time. You will often be surprised.

For instance, when I was researching this particular ebook I learned that I should be targeting people who want to "write a book", as much, or even more than, people wanting to "write an ebook"; something I wouldn't have known without conducting this online research.

This type of research also gave me valuable information on what else had been published on the same subject. This information was helpful in differentiating both my product and my book/ebook title from the competition.

So, don't even think about starting your book/ebook without first doing at least some basic demand/supply market research online.

Skip this critical step and you could go terribly wrong and end up writing a book/ebook on a topic about which no one is looking for information online.

STEP 2: BRAINSTORM YOUR TITLE

After you've done the background research to clarify the focus of your book/ebook, and you have some idea what the market and competition look like, you're ready to start working on a title.

And yes, it is important that you choose your final title now. It is required at this stage in order to drive a number of other activities that need to be initiated at this early phase.

Not only that – committing yourself to a final title at this point will really galvanize your focus for the rest of the process.

Having to decide on the final title now will also force you to do any other research that may be necessary at this point.

It's All About The Keywords

Without exception, if you plan to market your book or ebook through online distribution channels, including keywords and/or keyword phrases in your title and/ sub-title is absolutely essential.

You need to ensure that whatever title you develop includes your most important theme-related keywords/phrases to allow the search engines to find your book. This is critical since just about every search engine on the Net is keyword based.

Although the search engines use a variety of criteria to rank your website when a search is made, inclusion of your primary keywords is essential.

For example, the day I wrote this page I entered my number one search phrase "recommendation letter" into both www.google.com and www.yahoo.com search engines.

In both cases, my sites were returned in the first few positions. Take a look:
www.writinghelp-central.com/recommendation-letter.html
www.instantrecommendationletterkit.com/

Nevertheless, very few people are aware that inclusion of your essential keywords and/or keyword phrases in your title and sub-title will be even more critical when you start marketing your book through the online book portals such as amazon.com and barnesandnoble.com

Did I mention that you should have both a title AND a sub-title? Absolutely!

Create a short/punchy main title and a longer more descriptive sub-title. Using the two titles in tandem will give you more opportunity to include your primary keywords/phrases. As well, a longer more descriptive overall title will help you with your marketing efforts, both online and offline.

The search engines of online booksellers such as amazon.com and barnesandnoble.com will focus almost entirely on your title and sub-title. Even though amazon.com also uses its "search inside the book" search results technology, it still looks at the title and sub-title first.

A couple of relevant examples should make this point crystal clear. Consider the titles of one of my ebooks as follows:

"Instant Recommendation Letter Kit – How To Write Winning Letters of Recommendation"

It shouldn't be hard to see why I chose that title. It just so happens that the two most searched for terms on the subject of writing recommendation letters are "recommendation letter" and "letter of recommendation". Another highly ranked search term is "how to write a recommendation letter".

As you can see I've loaded my title/sub-title with the critical keywords.

To see this concept in action, go to www.amazon.com and do a book search on the phrase "recommendation letter".

Now try a book search at amazon.com using "letter of recommendation". Once again you'll see my book in the top 10 search results.

Let's look at one more example using another one of my ebooks:

"Instant College Admission Essay Kit – How To Write a Personal Statement Essay That Will Get You In"

In this case, keyword research revealed that the two most important search terms related to this subject were "college admission essay" and "personal statement".

Those two were closely followed by "admission essay" and "how to write a personal statement".

Again, I've loaded the title and sub-title with the relevant keywords.

Once again you can go to www.amazon.com and check out how this works.

Try doing book searches for the phrases "college admission essay" and "personal statement" and "personal statement essay".

The day I wrote this, my ebook came up in the top 5 of all three of these searches.

So, forget the "cutesy" titles like "Fixing Grandpa's Old Rocking Chair".

Instead, use something like "How To Fix Wooden Furniture In No Time Flat", because you've done the research and you know that "how to fix wooden furniture" is one of the top search phrases that people are using in your niche.

Hopefully I've made it crystal clear how critical it is to include your "most searched for keywords" in the title and sub-title of your book/ebook

Finalize Your Title

Did I mention how important it is to finalize your title at this stage so it is "cast in concrete" from this point on? I guess I did, but this point is so key I'm repeating it here one more time.

Your final title will be needed for the following four tasks that you need to do early in the process:

- registering your copyright (See pg. 61).
- obtaining your ISBN number (See pg. 62).
- registering your domain name (See pg. 64).
- ordering your cover (See pg. 67).

Not only that -- having a final title at this stage will really crystallize things and will help you focus on your book/ebook very specifically.

For me this definitely helps to make the writing process flow more easily.

STEP 3: GET YOUR TITLE REGISTERED

If you want your book/ebook to be taken seriously, and you want to keep your options open for various marketing channels, make sure you register your copyright and get your ISBN number assigned.

I've noticed that many ebook authors don't even bother to get their books properly copyrighted or obtain ISBN numbers for their books. This is either very short-sighted, or it may be due to sheer ignorance in some cases.

If you don't get your copyright registered you will have no legal rights should someone decide to use your material without permission.

Not getting an ISBN number will mean that the publishing community at large will never regard your book/ebook as the real thing -- you will not be taken seriously.

Even if you aren't sure at the beginning how far you will go with your book/ebook I highly recommend that you register the copyright and obtain the ISBN at this point so you won't regret later on that you didn't get them.

Get Your Book Copyrighted

Having your book/ebook title copyrighted means that you will be the only person who has the legal right to copy or reproduce that body of work. Your copyright gives you the exclusive right to publish or use your work in any number of ways.

Make sure you do this to protect yourself. It's worth the trouble and expense, if any, to protect your work. Do whatever is required in your country of residence.

Copyright laws vary from jurisdiction to jurisdiction but are very similar in intent and coverage. You'll have to see what specific laws and application process are applicable in the jurisdiction where you live.

For example, in Canada, where I live, the copyright on a written work usually exists for the life of the author and for 50 years thereafter.

To register a copyright in **Canada**, the Web address is:
http://strategis.ic.gc.ca/sc_mrksv/cipo/cp/cp_main-e.html

To apply for copyright registration in the **United States** go to:
http://www.copyright.gov/register/literary.html

On the other hand, some countries, such as the United Kingdom and Australia do not require one to register a copyright at all. They deem a copyright to be automatic the moment a work is recorded in any form.

Following are copyright info links for United Kingdom and Australia:

United Kingdom copyright information:
http://www.ipo.gov.uk/whatis/whatis-copy.htm

Australia copyright information:
http://www.copyright.org.au/information/basics.htm

In light of the above differences, make sure you check out the copyright laws and process in your own country of residence.

Make Sure You Get An ISBN Number

An International Standard Book Number (ISBN) is a numerical identification system used for books and other publications worldwide. It is a unique thirteen-digit number assigned to each published title and is recognized throughout the publishing industry internationally.

Publishers, distributors, booksellers, libraries and all other participants in the book industry use ISBNs to identify publications in order to expedite their handling and retrieval. ISBNs ensure that ordering, inventory control and accounting are executed more efficiently.

If you ever want your book/ebook to be distributed via any part of the international book publishing industry you will need an ISBN. Without an ISBN your book/ebook will not be recognized or processed by any publisher, bookseller, or library.

Here's where you can get ISBN's in various countries:

Canadian ISBN Agency:
http://www.collectionscanada.gc.ca/isn/index-e.html

United States ISBN Agency:
http://www.isbn.org/standards/home/isbn/us/application.asp

International ISBN Agency:
http://www.isbn-international.org/en/agencies.html

For residents of some countries, Canada for example, you can get an ISBN number for free. In other countries it will cost you. You will have to check in each case.

For example, in the United States you need to pay a publisher registration fee of $19.95 and then buy a minimum block of 10 ISBN numbers for a fee of $350.

Use the International ISBN link above to find out the situation in your own country.

ISBN Tip: *If you produce the same book for publication in two different formats (i.e. digital download and POD) you will need different ISBNs for each version.*

STEP 4: REGISTER YOUR DOMAIN NAME

Once you have finalized your title/sub-title and have protected your work to the extent possible with a copyright, it's time to register the domain name for your eventual website.

By domain name I'm referring to what's often referred to as a URL (for Universal Resource Locator). For example, www.yourebookdomainname.com is the format for a typical URL.

Ideally, your domain name will contain one of your primary keyword phrases and/or the short title of your book/ebook.

For example, for my ebooks I normally use the short title of my book as the domain name URL. For example:

http://www.instanthomewritingkit.com
http://www.instantrecommendationletterkit.com
http://www.instantbusinessletterkit.com
http://www.instantresignationletterkit.com

To Hyphenate Or Not…

Since I've been online there has been an ongoing debate as to whether you should hyphenate between keywords in your domain name to get better rankings with the search engines. I've read numerous conflicting opinions on this.

For instance, should one use: www.homefurniturestore.com or should it be www.home-furniture-store.com?

In my experience, neither approach will hurt you (i.e. with hyphens, or without).

One thing I do know for sure is that, as I write this, my *Instant Recommendation Letter Kit* site is ranked near the top at Yahoo! and that URL <u>does not</u> use hyphens.

I suggest you use what you think sounds and looks best, and will be easier for people to remember.

Stick With Dot Com

One other ongoing debate is whether you should get a ".com" suffix for your domain name, or one of the newer ones like ".net", ".org", ".biz", etc?

If you can get it, I recommend you use ".com" as your suffix. It is still the recognized business suffix. It will give you more credibility and people are less likely to get it wrong since it's the well-known gold standard.

Of course, if your site is non-profit and you want it to appear that way, by all means use ".org".

If ".com" isn't available and you don't want to adjust your URL, try ".net" as the next best thing. Nevertheless, if it were me, I would consider revising my URL keyword phrase before opting for ".net" or ".biz".

There are hundreds of domain registration services all over the Web. Watch out though, because some of them charge much more than others, for no value added.

Here are some reasonably-priced domain name services:

http://www.web.com
http://www.godaddy.com
http://www.123ehost.com

When I wrote this, the above three services were charging between $6.95 and $9.95 to register a single domain name for one year.

Don't ever pay more than $10 per URL.

To look at other choices go to <u>www.google.com</u> and enter "register domain name" and you'll find dozens more such services.

Domain Name Tip: *In order to simplify administration and to minimize the number of companies you have to deal with, I find it's a good idea to register your domain names through the same service that hosts your website (see Step 12, pg. 92).*

STEP 5: ORDER YOUR COVER

Even if you're producing a digital download ebook and will never be publishing a hard copy paperback version, you will still need a professionally designed book cover image for presentation and marketing purposes.

It is a well-known fact in the publishing industry that "covers sell books", and that's no different on the Net. In fact, it may be even truer online since potential buyers can't pick up your book and thumb through a copy as they can in a book store, so all they have is the visual image of the cover with which to relate.

Without a doubt, your book/ebook cover is the single most important marketing image you will ever have, both online and offline.

I suggest that you order your cover art right up-front, as soon as your title is fixed and your domain name set.

Although it won't actually be needed until the website goes online, I find that having the cover image posted up in front of me is a great help in stimulating the writing process.

In fact, as I sit here right now I'm looking up at my cover image for this ebook.

Hire A Professional Designer

Your cover design MUST be professional looking if your book is to have impact and credibility.

I'm continually amazed at some of the "cheesy" and amateurish looking cover designs I see all over the place as I surf around the Net.

What are these people thinking?

Clearly, if they have a tacky and unprofessional looking cover it will project exactly that same image about the quality of their book/ebook.

The cover is no place to skimp on the expenses folks! Especially, when you consider that you can get a high quality cover image online with all the bells and whistles for about $100 these days.

The "bells and whistles" will normally include: three or four 3D cover images of different sizes, a website header or masthead, a couple of flat cover images, and perhaps a banner image or two and an order button.

Cover Image Tip No 1: *I suggest you also request a large flat image about 600 pixels by 800 pixels to use as the cover page image in your digital download ebook This large opening image will have impact when people open your digital book.*

A number of times people have tried to sell me cover design software claiming that I could design my own covers and other website images. This is absolutely ridiculous! I am NOT a trained (or talented) graphic designer.

Don't waste your time. Hire a professional and get the job done properly!

Visualize Your Cover Concept

Although I advise strongly against you becoming a cover designer, it doesn't hurt to give your designer some conceptual ammunition to work with.

On a number of occasions I have visualized a rough cover design in my mind and passed that info on to the designer when I commissioned the job. I think that both the designer and I have found that helpful.

Let's face it, when you contact a cover designer he/she will not have had a chance to think about your book/ebook in advance. So if you can, give them an initial concept to work with. They'll likely appreciate it and will get a design back to you sooner.

For instance, when I was developing my ebook *Instant Resignation Letter Kit*, I had an image in my mind which I passed on to my designer, Ovi Dogar.

I told Ovi the scene I visualized for the cover was "…a professional man or woman standing at the threshold of a bridge at sunset, looking back and waving goodbye".

Here's the cover design Ovi came up with:

Of course, in the context of resignation letters, the "crossing over" into "brighter new horizons" is the obvious imagery here, but I was quite pleased with what Ovi came up with. I think he really brought my suggested concept to life, don't you?

Take a look at the Web site header:

http://www.instantresignationletterkit.com

Cover Image Tip No 2: *If you **ever** expect to offer your book as a print-on-demand (POD) paperback through amazon.com and/or others, ask your designer to produce 300 dpi cover images up-front. Normal Web images are 72 dpi and will not be acceptable for distribution to book sellers and distributors. So, if you get all images in 300 dpi up-front, you'll be killing two birds with one stone. Otherwise, you'll have to pay for additional 300 dpi images later.*

There are dozens of cover designers online, so you can shop around if you like.

My initial cover designer was Vaughan Davidson of New Zealand. Vaughan is a very talented designer and many of the top online gurus use his services: http://www.killercovers.com

I was very happy with the covers and headers Vaughan did for me but I found that he was getting overloaded with work and it was taking 5 to 7 days just to get a draft concept back from him. His prices went up as well. But he IS very good.

Then I ran across Ovi Dogar of Romania. Ovi is an excellent cover designer who bends over backwards to make his customers happy. He's also very fast and relatively inexpensive. I normally get a draft cover concept (or three!) back from Ovi within 24 hours; 48 hours at the most. http://www.absolutecovers.com

When I told Ovi I was writing this ebook he was kind enough to offer you a special discount. **Just tell Ovi in your e-mail that I sent you and he'll give you $10 off:** mailto:office@absolutecovers.com

If you want to do some cover graphics shopping just go to www.google.com and enter the phrases "book cover design" and/or "ebook cover design".

STEP 6: DECIDE ON KEY PARAMETERS

It will expedite the actual writing process later if you make some key decisions up-front regarding the "look and feel" of your ebook/book.

Step 6 is the best point to do this.

Spend some time with the word processing software you are going to use to create your book and do some layout experimentation.

Length Of Your Book

It's up to you, but I strongly recommend that you target for **at least 100 pages** for your book length from the outset. If you're going to be charging people good money for your book/ebook you've got to give them a reasonable amount of content (or at least the appearance of such).

Actually, there are some organizations in the international book publishing world that don't consider a document a "real book" unless it's at least 100 pages. Some other organizations accept 50 pages as the minimum.

In my opinion, anything under 100 pages is a "booklet" or "report" and will not be taken as seriously as a book. -- especially if you're trying to sell it. People will be much more willing to pay for a book as opposed to a booklet.

So, I always target for at least 100 pages at the beginning of the process and my book/ebook invariably ends up longer than that in any case.

Don't be daunted by that 100 pages figure. It's not as hard as you think, and there are a number of ways to stretch your book out, through crafty formatting. I'll get into that in more detail in Step 10. (See page 82).

Formatting Your Book

Formatting usually refers to page layout and includes the positioning of your top and bottom page margins as well as the format of your headers and footers.

The overall format I've used in this ebook you're reading right now is essentially the standard format that has evolved for me as I've developed my first dozen ebooks.

Create Your Template

I find that the most effective way to see what page format choices are best is to experiment using an actual document so I can "see" exactly what things look like.

So, open up your word processing program and create a template for your ebook. Now, experiment until you find a combination that you like. First set up your margins and then try different font style and size combinations.

Type/Font Style and Size

According to the experts, different font styles are either easier, or more difficult to read, depending on whether they are being read online (via screen monitor) or offline (via printed page).

Serif fonts	Sans-Serif fonts
Times	Arial
Georgia	Verdana
Garamond	Tahoma

The two main types of font styles are "serif" and "sans serif" As shown above, a serif font is one with little short and/or curly strokes at the ends of each part of a letter, while sans serif does not have these little strokes.

The experts have concluded that serif fonts are easier to read offline/printed; while sans serif fonts are easier on the eyes online/on-screen.

If you're writing an ebook your choice of font styles can be a bit tricky since it will likely be read both online and offline. So, which do you choose, serif or sans serif?

What I do, and what I suggest you consider doing, is to opt in favor of the offline option, serif, as your main font style, based on the following reasoning.

In my experience, people scan my ebooks online, but most also print them out and use the printed version as their main reference copy. Also, I normally issue a printed POD version of my ebooks eventually, which favors the serif option.

I once read somewhere that that the best combination is to use a serif font for your body text and a sans-serif font for the headings. Accordingly, I normally use Arial (sans serif) for my headings and Times New Roman (serif) for my text.

Of course, on my websites I always use the Verdana sans serif fonts.

As for font size, I typically use Times New Roman, 14 point, for my body text. I find that to be the perfect size for a highly readable book/ebook. A slightly larger size like this likely alleviates much of the strain of reading serif fonts online.

Line Spacing

For line spacing I use 1.5, or about 20 point. For this ebook I've used exactly 21 point line spacing (i.e. 14 x 1.5). This allows sufficient white space between lines to make the text easily readable without the lines seeming too far apart.

Choose whichever parameters work best for you. Just make sure you are consistent and keep readability as your number one priority.

Colors and Graphics

You can use color wherever you wish but don't overdo it and make things difficult to read. For example, in this ebook I use color for my headings and sub-headings and that's all. These appear as different shades of black and gray in my POD books.

I generally don't use artwork graphics in my ebooks. I tend to be conservative and so my books tend to be very businesslike due to their practical toolkit nature.

I do know of a couple of Internet marketing "gurus" who use cutesy little graphics liberally throughout their ebooks. Nice, but not necessary. It's the content that really counts.

Again, do what works best for you and your target audience. Here are a couple of free clip art sites that can get you started if you want to go that route.
http://www.barrysclipart.com/
http://www.clip-art.com

Headers and Footers

I always use page headers and footers for the types of books/ebooks that I produce because I believe they give a more professional and crisp look to both the page and the document as a whole.

I generally recommend that you use page headers and footers too.

Once you've made your formatting choices, create a master document template in your word processing program and save it with all of the settings you have chosen enabled. Use that document from now on as your master document template.

Bottom line: *Be as creative as you want with your ebook format. Just remember to keep readability as your number one priority.*

STEP 7: DEVELOP TABLE OF CONTENTS

If you've ever read any of my articles about report writing you'll know that I'm a big believer in the development of an organized outline <u>before</u> you start to write.

In fact, I am adamant that you should develop at least the draft version of your book/ebook's Table of Contents (TOC) right up-front.

The following section is a slightly modified excerpt from one of my articles on the subject of business report writing.

Write The Table of Contents First

In my experience, drafting the actual Table of Contents, before you start writing the actual book/ebook is the single most important key to developing a successful document.

This should normally be done before, or in parallel with, the first phase of project information gathering.

This needs to be more than just a rough draft TOC. It should be a carefully thought out breakdown of exactly what you imagine the TOC will look like in your final book/ebook. Although this takes a certain amount of time and brain power up-front, it really streamlines the rest of the process.

What I do is to actually visualize the final report in my mind's eye and then write down the contents outline.

If you can, try to at least develop your chapter or section headings, plus the first set of sub-headings under each one of those. Be sure to do this in your word processing program so that your TOC outline will be the first version of your book/ebook.

Make sure you use the master document template that you created at the end of Step 6 which should already have your formatting all set up. (See pg. 72).

Creating the Blueprint For Your Book

Once you've opened your new book/ebook document in your word processing program, start entering each of the headings and sub-headings in the same sequence in which they'll appear in your book.

Leave a few blank lines/spaces between each heading/sub-heading.

When you've entered all of them and marked them as headings and sub-headings, as per your word processor's styles table, go to the beginning of the document and generate an automatic Table of Contents.

Normally, this "auto generate a table of contents" will be a standard function in your word processing program. Although, the exact procedure for generating an automatic TOC will depend on which word processing software you're using.

For instance, to do this in MS-Word you would click on the following sequence of dropdown menu selections from the main toolbar:

Insert/Reference/Index and Tables/Table of Contents

This will automatically insert your Table of Contents as the first page in the page sequence of your document.

The resulting document will be a one-page Table of Contents followed by one or more pages of headings and sub-headings with blank lines between them.

For example, the three (3) pages of the resulting document will look something like the following example when you've finished the above exercise:

Please note that the following is a fictitious example, invented for illustration purposes. It does not relate directly to any particular document, including this one.

Page 2

Introduction

Background

Assumptions

Chapter 1 – Researching

Study Your Niche

Seek Out Your Source Material

Create Research Summaries

Page 3

Chapter 2 – Writing

Create Your Outline

Draft Each Chapter

Review and Revise

Chapter 3 – Getting Published

Submit Your Manuscript

Making the Follow-Up Calls

Reacting To An Offer

Conclusion

The resulting document now becomes your "blueprint" or skeleton outline for the actual writing process.

I urge you to try this process as described above. It really does work!

STEP 8: DEVELOP DETAILED CONTENT POINTS

Once you have produced your Table of Contents outline as shown in the previous step there is one more thing you need to do before you start the actual writing.

First, print out your master Table of Contents outline document that you just created, or open it into a new window in your word processing program.

Drill Down One More Level

What you want to do now is to go down one more level of detail <u>below</u> the headings/sub-headings level of detail that you've already identified above.

Working through your outline from the beginning, one heading/sub-heading at a time, "brainstorm" and list all of the main points that you want to cover in that section.

These "content points", as I call them, are not sub-headings at this point, although some may become sub-headings later. They are essentially notes to yourself.

At this stage the "content points" are just a point-form list of subjects and/or "working notes" on what you want to be sure to cover when you get to that particular sub-section of your document during the writing process. For example:

Page 2

Introduction
Background
- explain why I'm writing this
- identify target audience

Assumptions
- identify timeframe covered
- explain what is not covered
- talk about the pilot project
- outline phases 2 and 3
- identify funding levels assumed

The bulleted points in the above example are your actual "content points" that you will use to guide you in developing your material during the actual writing process.

Once you have all of your "content points" listed on the second version of the outline, print that document. You now have your detailed book/ebook outline.

Now, post that document directly in your line-of-sight and follow along with it as you write your book/ebook.

After you begin writing from the content points you'll notice as you go along that some of the points will make good logical headings, either at the same level as the sub-headers already identified, or below those sub-headers. If the latter is the case you will want to introduce one more level of headings to your document.

For, example, you will notice that this particular document actually has four (4) different levels of headings. Only three of those are listed in the Table of Contents, but there is a 4th level included in some chapters.

Writing Tip: *In addition to posting your detailed outline in your line-of-sight, before you start writing, I suggest you gather together as much of the research material that you will need to consult and make sure it is also nearby. This way you'll have everything you need close-at-hand and won't have to interrupt the writing process for too long when you need to refer to something. What I often do is put all of my background documents into a three-ring binder and keep that binder right beside me for quick reference when I'm writing. This technique works very well for me. I find that once I get into "writing mode" any distractions such as having to search for background documents that I've already collected, break my concentration and throw me off-track and slow down the entire process.*

STEP 9: WRITE YOUR BOOK/EBOOK

I don't mean to be too cute here folks, but if you've followed my advice so far, at this point the writing process should be almost like filling-in-the-blanks.

That's right. Because you've done all the preparation in Steps 7 and 8, the actual writing process should be relatively straightforward.

Your Writing Tools

During this phase, your two main tools for writing your book/ebook will be:

- The formatted master document template (from Step 6) with the Table of Contents outline at the beginning, as you developed and saved it in your word processing program in Step 7. (See pg. 76).

- The detailed content points outline that you developed and printed out as a reference document in Step 8. (See pg. 79).

The actual writing process should be a relatively simple matter of filling-in-the-blanks because you will have a fully-formatted template to work with—the TOC and document outline you already developed in Step 7.

In addition, you'll also have the detailed point-form breakdown of the specific subjects/content points you want to cover that you created in Step 8. All you have to do is follow along with that as you write.

The Writing Process

It's very straightforward. Using the writing tools described above, just start at the very beginning of your book/ebook and keep on writing until you get to the end.

I really love the actual writing part when I do things the way I've described above.

By the time I get to this stage I've done all of the thinking and leg work. I find it's really invigorating because the words just seem to "flow" at this point, with all of the preparation done and any needed references close at hand.

It's almost like being in "automatic writing mode".

This approach truly does eliminate a lot of the "pain" from the writing process.

Notes On Formatting

Since you will be working with the draft Table of Contents that you created in Step 7, the formatting of your document template should be all set up based on the formatting choices that you made in Step 6.

In review -- In Step 6 you will have already selected settings for: page margins, font style and size for headings and body text, header/footer formats, and line spacing.

With all of that already decided (Step 6) and applied (Step 7) there are only two other formatting considerations during the actual writing phase – paragraph length and page breaks, as follows…

Paragraph Length

To make your book/ebook less dense and more readable make sure you leave lots of white space by using lots of breaks between paragraphs. Generally speaking, paragraph length should never exceed two to three sentences. Note how I've done it in this book/ebook.

Page Breaks

Another way to reduce density and improve readability is to use lots of page breaks at logical points in your text. For instance, I generally skip to a new page at each of my first two levels of headings.

STEP 10: EDIT AND REVISE YOUR BOOK

As described in Step 9, write the first draft of your book page by page, section by section, and chapter by chapter -- starting at page one and then working your way through to the end, one-page-at-a-time.

Light Edit During Writing Process

While doing your first draft don't spend a lot of time editing and revising. Focus on getting your thoughts written down.

If you've followed the recommended preparation steps already covered, you won't have to worry too much about getting off track as you go along.

After all, you've already organized your thoughts using the headings/sub-headings and then broken it down even further with the detailed content points.

When doing the first pass I usually do a quick scan as I complete writing each page and make any minor revisions that jump out at me. Otherwise, I leave it until later.

Major Edits After First Draft

When you've completed the first draft, do a line-by-line on-screen edit in your word processing program.

During this phase use your word processor's spell checker and grammar checker to pick up anything obvious.

Check the number of pages at this point. Is your draft document long enough? Remember, you want to shoot for at least 100 pages.

If it's too short, make some minor adjustments to left/right margins and adjust the standard text line spacing. You'd be surprised at how this will increase the length of your document

Document Length Tip: *I just did a test using a 90 page MS-Word document. I simply increased the"Normal" line-spacing point size from 20 to 22 and decreased the right margins by 1/8" and the page count increased by a full 9 pages!*

Once you're satisfied with your online edit; print out the entire book/ebook.

I usually print out one copy and give it to a friend of mine who once worked as an editor with a major magazine publisher. She then goes through the document in detail and marks-up any problems she sees on the hard copy.

Once I get her marked-up hard copy back, I then sit down with a pen and go through the entire document one final time, line-by-line, adding any final edits of my own to the hard copy.

Using that copy, marked-up by both me and my friend, I sit down to do my final on-screen edit, page-by-page.

Online Editing Resources

Not everyone has a friend who is capable of doing a thorough editorial review for them. But don't worry about that. There are hundreds of editors and editing services online that can help you.

One service that I've had personal contact with is George Robinson's WritingEnglish.com which offers English proofreading and editing services. http://www.writingenglish.com

Someone I have personal experience working with who offers excellent editorial and proofreading services is Lauren Hidden of Hidden Helpers:

http://www.hiddenhelper.com

In addition, there are literally hundreds and hundreds of writing and editorial services available online. One well-known and trusted source is elance.com:

http://www.elance.com

Look there under the "Writing & Translation" category and you will find scores of writers and/or editors willing to bid on your editing job.

And if that doesn't give you enough choices, go to www.google.com and enter the phrase "editing services" and hundreds of sites will pop up.

Editing Tip: *Being a Canadian, I use Canadian English spelling and grammar in my day-to-day life. Nevertheless, I always make sure that my spell checker and grammar checker are both set to "U.S. English" when writing/editing my books/ebooks for the simple reason that about 90% of my customers are U.S.-based. Besides, these days it seems that U.S. English has become the de facto online standard.*

STEP 11: CREATE/PUBLISH YOUR EBOOK

Once you've finished your final edit it's now time to actually "publish" your book/ebook in a form that everyone can read online.

Up until this point you have been writing and editing your masterpiece in your word processing program. Typically, this involves word processing programs such as MS-Word (Microsoft) or WordPerfect (Corel), or something equivalent.

It's now time to convert your word processing document into a real ebook, or digital download book.

Publishing Tip: *Make sure that you do ALL formatting that you want in your final document while you're still in your word processing program. There's no point also getting into formatting in your PDF conversion process. If you do that, it will mean that you'll have to buy more sophisticated and expensive PDF conversion software when it's not really necessary.*

PDF -- The Only Way To Go

As I clearly and unequivocally stated in the Assumptions section of the Introduction to this book, these days there is only one universally accepted standard for publishing ebooks -- Adobe's portable document format (PDF). (See page 44).

Until I knew how to do this conversion myself I was quite intimidated by the whole idea of converting my source files into PDF format. It sounded very "techie" and I therefore avoided it at first.

In fact, I was so intimidated, that I paid someone else who owned a copy of the Adobe Publisher software to convert my first three ebooks into PDF for me!

Now that I know how simple it is (Yes, even for non-techies!) I just shake my head.

At least that person didn't charge me too much. Of course, now that I know what's actually involved I also know that he didn't have to do very much either.

As I was saying, the Adobe Corporation is the company responsible for inventing PDF format. PDF has three great things going for it, as follows:

- **PDF documents are completely portable** from platform to platform so they can be read on any computer system (i.e. Windows-based, Mac-based, and others), using an Adobe supplied reader (free software).

- **PDF documents are 100% WYSIWYG** (What You See Is What You Get). This means that the document that you created in your source word processing software will appear in PDF exactly as you created it, with exactly the same fonts, formats, spacing, graphics, etc. (Not the case with other ebook creators).

- **PDF Reader software is free** to anyone who chooses to download it from Adobe's website. The software downloads easily and normally installs on your computer automatically. These days, it seems like the vast majority of computer users have a copy of Adobe Reader already installed on their computer.

Of course, for you to be reading this as an ebook you will have Adobe Reader currently installed on your computer. In any case, here's the URL for the download: http://www.adobe.com/products/acrobat/readstep2.html

PDF Creation Software

As I stated above, I was so spooked by the prospect of having to convert my MS-Word masterpiece into PDF format that I actually paid someone to do it for me the first few times.

On the other hand, I don't like being dependent on others for every little thing, so eventually my need to be self-contained overcame my fear of PDF technology.

So I did some research into what was available and came up with the following:

When it comes to PDF creation software Adobe Corporation rules.

It is currently offering Adobe Acrobat X.0 (Standard) for US $299.
http://www.adobe.com/products/acrobatstd/main.html

Adobe also offers Acrobat X.0 (Professional) at $449, but that's for the real pros.

As I write this, Adobe is also offering an online service that allows users to convert documents to PDF on a subscription basis, for $9.99 per month or $99. per year.
https://createpdf.adobe.com/cgi-feeder.pl/sublevels?BP=IE&LOC=en_US

At that same link they also offer a free trial service that allows you to convert five (5) pages to PDF at a time, for no charge.

I considered buying Adobe Acrobat (Standard) but decided against it because I felt that it had way more functionality (i.e. features) than I need when I only have to convert three (3) or four (4) documents per year into PDF files.

I have no doubt that Adobe Acrobat is the gold standard in PDF creation software but I felt it would be overkill for my relatively simple needs (assuming that I could find a reasonable substitute of course).

After a couple of false starts with other PDF creation products, the details of which I won't go into here, I was lucky enough to find a great PDF creation program:

It's called PDF Factory and it's produced by Fine Print Inc. There are two main versions of their software, pdfFactory ($49.95) and pdfFactoryPro ($99.95).
http://www.pdffactory.com/products/pdffactory/index.html

I opted for the latter because it has security features and creates "bookmarks" as a clickable index in my documents.

As I said, I have been very pleased with pdfFactoryPro since I bought it. In fact, I used it to create the document that you're reading right now.

If you go to www.google.com and enter "pdf creation software" you will find links to at least 10 to 15 other PDF creation software programs.

Here's a PDF Creator that I just came across recently that looks interesting. I haven't used it myself though. It's called PDF Converter Professional 5 ($99.99). http://www.nuance.com/pdfconverter/professional/

Shop around and go with what you think offers best value for your needs.

PDF Software Tip: *When I was researching PDF creation software I had a few surprises. I found a couple of basic PDF creation packages that were quite inexpensive and I thought that they could do the job. However, after testing, neither one was acceptable. One program wouldn't allow the embedding (inclusion) of all of the fonts used in my original MS-Word documents. The other program didn't convert MS-Word clickable hyperlinks into clickable hyperlinks in the pdf document. Both of these are serious flaws. So, before you choose a PDF conversion package, test it and make sure it gives you everything you need.*

Other Formats Emerging

Although PDF format is the only way to go at the time I am writing the Revised Edition of this book/ebook; there are some market forces that are trying to establish wider acceptance of some alternative formats. This issue is discussed in some detail earlier in the Introduction to the 17 Action Steps. (See page 45).

STEP 12: CREATE YOUR SALES-MINI-SITE

Once you've created your ebook in PDF format you're ready to sell it online.

Based on everything I've learned in the past half-dozen few years, there is only one way to effectively sell a product such as an ebook online.

A Mini-Site Is A Must

You MUST have a dedicated sales-mini-site to sell your ebook effectively.

To verify this, just look at what the most successful Internet marketers do whenever they release a new product – they create a dedicated sales-mini-site.

> I learned about the necessity of single product focused mini-sales-sites back when I was a newbie, and "guru-guy" had me convinced that all I had to do to make a living online was set-up a theme-based content site and start collecting those affiliate commission checks. (See page 13). Well, it wasn't long before I realized I needed to develop my own products if I was ever going to have a hope of making a living online. So, I developed my first theme-related ebook and placed it on my theme-based content site. Sales didn't exactly take off. That's when I discovered that no matter how hard I tried, I couldn't get more than 35% of those targeted visitors to click on my ebook link. It turned out that my free content was competing directly with my ebook! Not good. It was then that I sought out other gurus who showed me that sales-mini-sites were the only way to go. Now, when people come to my mini-sites, all 100% of those targeted visitors are potential buyers, and my site copy is 100% focused on converting them into actual buyers.

A sales-mini-site is a dedicated website with a URL specific to the product being sold on that site. The entire purpose of that sales-mini-site is to provide specific information to visitors about the one product being sold there with the ultimate objective of converting a certain percentage of those visitors from "browsers" to "buyers" before they leave that site.

For examples of sales-mini-sites, you can look at any one of these sites:
http://www.instanthomewritingkit.com
http://www.instantrecommendationletterkit.com
http://www.instantbusinessletterkit.com
http://www.instantresignationletterkit.com
http://www.instantcollegeadmissionessay.com

I'm sure you'll see that each one of those sites has one purpose and one purpose only – to convince the targeted visitor to purchase the particular ebook being offered.

For your information, I modeled my first sales-mini-site on Yanik Silver's Instant Sales Letters website:
http://www.instantsalesletters.com

Yanik's site is a classic example of a successful sales-mini-site which is focused on a single product. Almost a decade after its creation, it still sells quite successfully.

There are of course, literally thousands of sales-mini-sites just like that one, offering thousands of products across the Internet, one-product-at-a-time.

So, if you seriously want to sell your ebook online you MUST have one of these.

And the good news is that creating and maintaining a sales-mini-site is not expensive, and not particularly difficult to set-up.

For example, to host each of my mini-sites listed above costs me less than US $75 per year, per site. That's the equivalent of 2 to 3 ebook sales.

Getting Your Mini-Site Hosted

In case you don't know or aren't clear about it, a Web Host is simply a company that will rent you online access to disk space and related resources and tools on their server (computer) on a monthly or yearly basis.

Of course, in your case, you'll likely be buying Web hosting services for the URL domain name that you already chose earlier in Step 4. (See page 64).

There are literally thousands of Web hosting companies. Just go to www.google.com and enter "web hosting" and you'll see what I mean. It's a competitive business.

There are so many of them I can't really tell you which one to go with. However, as a minimum for a sales-mini-site, you need the following from a Web host:

Host Service/Capability	Minimum Requirement
Disk Space	100 MB
Data Transfer rate	5 GB per month
E-mail	Unlimited accounts
Scripting support	CGI, PHP
Control panel (multi-function)	Direct user-friendly interface
Support	E-mail and telephone 24/7

You should be able to get the above minimum capabilities for anywhere between US $3.95 and $6.95per month at any one of dozens of Web hosting companies. No matter what, DO NOT PAY more than $8.95 per month for basic mini-site hosting.

In case you're wondering, I use one Web hosting company for all of my mini-sites: http://www.123ehost.com

I came across that company by chance a few years ago when I was doing some online web host pricing research. Their prices and features looked good, and by total fluke they are located in a suburb of Montreal! (So, I figured that if I had problems I could always drive over there and kick down their door!).

As it turned out I've been very happy with that company to-date. My sites rarely go down and the odd time when I have a question or problem their e-mail and phone support is excellent.

When I told Sam at 123ehost, that I was writing this book he gave me a link and told me that **anyone buying Web hosting from this link will get a $10 discount:** http://www.123ehost.com/ebook.htm

Web Hosting Tip: *No matter how tempting it may seem DO NOT use free Web hosting. Typically, you won't be able to use your own stand-alone URL, and the search engines will not take your site seriously. Potential customers will wonder too.* Don't risk it. It's not worth the definite downsides to save $60 to $75 per year.

Write Your Mini-Site Sales Copy

As I've already stated, the sole purpose of your sales-mini-site is to get your visitors to buy your book/ebook.

The key to getting them to buy is your sales copy of course.

If you're good at duplicating what others do, you may well decide to write your own sales copy using the examples of others. There are so many good ones out there.

But I warn you, online copywriting is an art in itself and it doesn't always follow the rules of offline copywriting. That being said, I write all of my own sales copy for my websites.

My sales copy may not be perfect but I've tried hard to emulate the techniques of some of the best copywriters on the Web. Let's say I'm an 8 out of 10 when compared with the copywriting gurus. That's good enough for me right now.

I'm not going to give you a course on sales copywriting here. There are complete books/ebooks written on that, and so-called copywriting gurus are constantly offering two and three day seminars on the subject.

One book that's considered to be among the very best on this subject is *"Make Your Words Sell"* by Ken Evoy and Joe Robson:
http://myws.sitesell.com/

On the other hand, if you decide that you don't want to write your own sales copy there are many who will do it for you -- for a fee of course.

One of the very best "for-hire" Web copy writers that I know of is a chap named Michel Fortin, aka "The Success Doctor":
http://successdoctor.com/

His work is excellent, but it ain't cheap! Make sure you have your check book handy when you contact him.

Another option is www.elance.com which lists hundreds of such resources under the categories *Writing & Translation* and *Web Design & Development*.

On average, my standard sales pages are about 3,000 words in length and go for 10 to 15 pages (8 ½" x 11") when printed out.

Nevertheless, since you will have already written a book/ebook, you should be able to do a pretty decent job of writing your own mini-site sales copy.

I suggest you study the copy on a few good mini-sites and try it yourself.

Here are a few sales-mini-sites with what I consider to be excellent sales copy:
http://www.33daystoonlineprofits.com
http://www.quitsmokingrightnow.com
http://www.superaffiliatehandbook.com

These are just a few sites that come to mind right now. There are hundreds of other excellent examples out there. You might want to check out some of my sites as well:
http://www.writinghelptools.com

Click on any of my book covers on that page and you'll be taken to the sales site.

Set-Up Your Payment Processing Account

The final step in getting your sales-mini-site "sales ready" will be to set-up an account with a company that offers payment processing services on behalf of webmasters.

A "payment processor" is a Web-based company that will handle secure credit card payments for you in exchange for a percentage of the sale. The major payment processors are able to handle all major credit cards plus online checks.

Typically, when a buyer clicks on one of the "order" links on your ebook sales site they will be taken to a secure Web server owned and managed by the payment processing company.

ClickBank

For all of my mini-sites I've used ClickBank as my payment processor almost from the very beginning. They specialize in digital download products.
http://www.clickbank.com

I believe that ClickBank is one of the largest payment processors on the Internet for small Web merchants. They claim to have over 10,000 merchant clients and an affiliate network exceeding 100,000. They process all major credit cards, as well as e-checks, and PayPal payments.

As I write this, ClickBank charges a flat fee of $1 per transaction plus 7.5% of the sale. That works out to about 11% on a $25 sale, or $2.80. On average, they take about 10% to 12 % of every sale depending on the price, so it isn't all that cheap.

But when you consider how easy they make it, and the fact that they're the only "middleman", it's not too bad.

One big plus with ClickBank is that they have a built-in affiliate program which allows other people to easily set up affiliate links that will send their visitors to your websites.

Overall I've found ClickBank to be excellent. There have been a few hiccups along the way, but nothing major. Their service is clean and easy to implement on your site and the checks keep coming in the mail every two weeks, just like clockwork.

PayPal

Another payment processing solution that many people use is PayPal.
http://www.paypal.com

In fact, PayPal was the first solution I tried for my first mini-site years ago. Unfortunately, at that time PayPal was having serious customer support problems so I dropped them in a hurry. I believe they have long since rectified those problems.

PayPal is very inexpensive. To receive/process payments from your Web site they charge a $0.30 transaction fee plus between 1.9% and 2.9% on each sale.

The one slight downside to PayPal (which is not insignificant) is that a user (i.e. your buyer) must register with PayPal before their payment will be accepted. This can be a barrier to sales, although many people are already registered since the company claims to have over 50 million users.

PayPal says it will accept payments from more than 190 countries:
http://www.paypal.com/cgi-bin/webscr?cmd=p/gen/approved_countries-outside

Nevertheless, even if you don't use PayPal as your payment processor I suggest you set up a standard user account with them. It's a very handy way of sending and receiving money online.

Even though I don't have a merchant account with PayPal anymore, I often use the service to pay suppliers who provide services to me for a fee. And a number of companies send me monthly affiliate commissions via PayPal.

PayPal allows you to send money to any valid e-mail address for no fee.

DigiBuy

Another company that quite a few people use for payment processing related to digital download products is DigiBuy.
http://www.digibuy.com

I know some webmasters who have been quite happy with their service.

Although, I just noticed that DigiBuy's standard fee is 13.9% of the sale. That's almost $3.50 on a $25 sale. Compared with ClickBank that's fairly pricey.

To check out additional payment processors go to www.google.com and enter "payment processing". You'll find a number of alternatives.

Design, Create and Upload Your Web Site

Once you've got your website hosted, you've written your sales copy, and you've signed-up with a payment processor, you're just about ready to go "live".

The only thing that remains to be done is to have your sales page converted into HTML (Hyper Text Mark-up Language) so that it can be read in people's browsers.

You Can Do it Yourself

If you know HTML you can do this part yourself.

Even if you don't know HTML, it is quite a simple language to learn and apply, so if you're open to the idea, try learning it for yourself.

In case you're interested, here are a couple of free HTML courses:
http://www.draac.com/html.html
http://webdesign.about.com/c/ec/9.htm

Web Design Tip: *One reason why you might want to try learning some basic HTML at this point is so that you won't have to rely on someone else for help every time you decide to tweak your sales copy or make minor additions/deletions. Knowing basic HTML to handle these types of things could save you considerable time, trouble and expense later.*

You Can Hire A Web Designer

On the other hand, if you don't want to learn HTML for yourself, no problem.

Again, you can go to www.elance.com and you'll find lots of help there under the *Web Design & Development* category.
http://www.elance.com/c/search/main/lSearch.pl?domain=profiles&mode=browse&stage=results&catid=10225

In fact, when I checked at the above link, more than 17,000 Web & Programming designers and services were listed, along with the rates they charge. So, if you submit your job particulars at that site you're bound to receive lots of bids.

You Can Look Close To Home

One other option to consider for basic Web design and HTML coding is checking out what's available in your local community.

Lots of high school and college kids these days know HTML and basic Web design techniques. Try posting your needs on the bulletin boards at those institutions.

Or, check with your friends and neighbors. Just about everyone will know of someone who can do a basic website for you. (Just make sure you have a professionally-designed model for the selected person to follow).

To sell a book/ebook online you don't need a flashy site with a lot of graphics. Just good solid sales copy focused on benefits, and targeting your visitors, will do it.

The only graphics you'll need are a header/masthead for the top of your sales page, and the cover image to insert once into your sales copy. You got those graphics done already in Step 5 (See page 67), so the only thing you have to do is transfer those files to whomever is doing your website design for you.

For typical examples of sales-mini-sites for ebooks you can check out any of the links on my WritingHelpTools Web site.
http://www.writinghelptools.com

Once your copy has been converted into HTML and combined with your graphic images, it needs to be uploaded to your website. Your website is the space you rent on your Web host's computer and is identified by your unique URL.

If you have hired someone to code your HTML they will normally upload it for you. Otherwise your Web host company will most likely offer a point and click FTP option from your control panel which just about anyone can do.

That's it! Once your webpage is uploaded to your website, you're ready to start selling ebooks!

Web Design Resources

There are literally thousands of websites offering tips, techniques and information about how to do Web design and coding. To see what I mean you can go to www.google.com and enter "web design help".

One excellent resource that I have discovered is Shelley Lowery's website: http://www.web-source.net

Shelley offers an amazing amount of free advice, information and code "snippets" on her site. It's my one-stop resource whenever I need help with HTML or JAVA scripts for my websites. Really, you don't have to look beyond Shelley's site.

Shelley has also written the definitive Web design and development book... *Web Design Mastery.* You can check it out at the following link: http://www.webdesignmastery.com/

If you're interested in buying Shelley's book, come back here to order it.

Shelley has provided the following $10 discount link for *Web Design Mastery*: http://www.clickbank.net/sell.cgi?wsnet/6/Web_Design_Mastery

STEP 13: LAUNCH YOUR BOOK/EBOOK

As soon as your website is online you'll want to undertake a few preliminary marketing activities just to get the ball rolling.

Get Those Testimonials

First of all, send a copy of your ebook to trusted experts in your field and ask them if they would consider providing you with a testimonial in exchange for a mention and possibly a link from your sales site to their website.

You will probably have your own short-list of experts who you can approach. In addition, you can do a bit of online research and look for webmasters offering products or services that are complimentary to yours. Add them to your list.

Of course, I don't recommend sending your ebook to your direct competition. If they want to find out what you're up to, they can at least buy it!

If you're uncomfortable with sending the actual ebook to a stranger out-of-the-blue, you can always send them a link to your website sales copy. Ask them to take a look at the site copy, and then to let you know if they would like you to send them a copy of the actual ebook. In exchange for a testimonial of course!

Getting a few good testimonials that you can post on your website is important. This will give you and your ebook credibility and will show your visitors that people have looked at your ebook and liked what they saw.

Post these testimonials on your site as soon as you get them.

For examples of typical testimonials, take a look at any of the example sites I mentioned in Step 12. Or you can try any of the links at:
http://www.writinghelptools.com

Here's a typical e-mail that I send out to webmasters requesting a testimonial:

Hi Veronica,

I just released my latest "writing help" eBook last week.

I was wondering if you would be interested in taking a look at a copy of the ebook and possibly giving me a testimonial. (If you find it to your liking of course). It's called:

"Instant College Admission Essay Kit - How To Write A Personal Statement Essay That Will Get You In"

This product gives buyers a low-cost, quality solution for putting together a decent draft BEFORE they go to a service such as yours. OR, for the rare applicant that is an excellent writer and/or is strapped financially, they could use my eBook to bypass editorial services if they so choose.

Using my solution should save people time, trouble and lots of money when developing their essay. They will end up with a quality draft essay or personal statement to submit to the essay editing services for final review and revision.

For example, I have developed a set of unique "essay preparation tools" to help applicants plan/develop their essay.

Also, the book is filled with numerous stern warnings against plagiarism. It even shows them how to use an existing essay template to fast-track their own, without copying.

Veronica, please let me know if you think you'll have the time to do a quick review of the eBook and I'll send you a copy.

Thanks in advance for your consideration.

All the best,

Shaun Fawcett, M.B.A.
1-800-600-6550 (toll-free)

In this case, the e-mail is going to a respected authority in the field about which the ebook is written. Because of that, I didn't want to be presumptuous and send a copy without her requesting it first. Make sure you use a personalized approach for each testimonial request that you send. Your response rate will be much better.

Make Special Offers

A great way to announce your new ebook is through special introductory offers.

You may have a mailing list of customers and/or a subscription list for a newsletter or catalog. Even if you don't have either of those, you're sure to have at least a personal contacts list.

Whenever I launch a new ebook, one of the first things I do is send an e-mail to everyone on my newsletter mailing list as well as to my personal list announcing the new book and making them a special offer.

My Special Introductory Offer is typically 25% to 30% off of the regular price.

Make sure you give them a deadline. It should be a "limited time" offer which compels them to take action by a certain date, or they'll miss out. Give them two or three days – no more than a week.

I find these Special Introductory Offers to be quite effective and they normally generate a decent number of up-front sales that I wouldn't otherwise get from my website.

As a minimum, those initial sales should cover the costs of Web hosting for a couple of years, and maybe the cover and website artwork costs as well.

Many of the Internet Marketing gurus issue a final appeal reminder e-mail about 24 hours or so before the offer time-limit expires. I've tried this and in most cases a few additional sales do straggle in as a result.

The important thing is to perform the above activities when your ebook is relatively "hot-off-the-press", so to speak.

Here's a typical "Special Introductory Offer" e-mail for one of my writing kits:

Hi Jackie,

YOU are receiving this Exclusive Mailing because you subscribed to the F-r-e-e Job Search Kit Series that Kevin Donlin and I have been offering from my Web site, WritingHelp-Central.com.

Two weeks ago I released my latest "writing kit" eBook, "Instant Resignation Letter Kit". http://instantresignationletterkit.com/cgi-bin/a/t.cgi?spnl

At that time I made a very special introductory offer to all of my newsletter subscribers. Later, it occurred to me that I should also make this one-time special deal available to everyone who participated in the Fr*e Job Kit series as well.

Here's a quick summary of the Kit, Jackie.

As you probably know, a Resignation Letter can be delicate and sensitive to write. You don't want to go too far, yet you want to cover everything that's required and say all the appropriate things.

I won't go into the details of all of the features and benefits of the Kit in this e-mail since I've prepared a Special Product Briefing Page especially for YOU. (I'll give you that link in a few seconds).

Here's just a little teaser to stir your interest...

If you need to know how to write ANY type of Resignation Letter for ANY situation this eBook is for you. It uses the standard "Instant Writing Toolkit" winning formula, combining comprehensive "how to" information with a wide range of "real-life" templates.

In fact, this Kit includes 39 "real-life" templates! 27 of them are Resignation letter templates, and 12 are post-resignation templates that one would normally need after the resignation.

Post-resignation templates include: resume cover letters, recommendation letters, reference letters, introduction letters, thank you letters, AND resignation retraction letters just in case you change your mind.

In addition, since most resignation situations involve one having to find a new position of some sort, I spent many hours researching the best online "Job Hunting" sites/services and have included the results in the Kit:

- Top 25 Career/Job Search Sites
- Top 25 Resume Writing Sites
- Top 25 Recommendation Letter Resources

- Top 25 Resignation Information Sites

This feature alone will save owners of the Kit many hours of tedious and often unproductive online research.

Jackie, as I said, I first put this special offer together with my newsletter subscribers in mind. Then I thought, "why not my Job Search Kit people too?"

So, here's your link to that Special Briefing Page...
http://instantresignationletterkit.com/cgi-bin/a/t.cgi?spnl

DON'T DELAY Jackie. As you'll see on the Special Product Briefing Page...
THIS OFFER EXPIRES IN A FEW DAYS.

All the best,

Shaun Fawcett, M.B.A.
P.S.
Of course my usual Guarantee is included! I'm so confident that the real-life templates in the Kit will cover 99.9% of your resignation letter writing needs, that I'll write you a letter from scratch if the Kit doesn't cover it!
http://instantresignationletterkit.com/cgi-bin/a/t.cgi?spnl

This particular e-mail went out to a special mailing list that I maintain that is made up of people who have signed-up for a special job search kit.

If you try the link in the above e-mail you'll see that it goes to a specially customized sales page created for people clicking through to the special offer. Of course, all of the order links on that page go to the special discount price.

E-mail Sales Tip: *Whenever you're sending any type of offer by e-mail DO NOT include the actual price in the e-mail itself. Use the e-mail to do some pre-selling and to arouse the reader's curiosity. If the recipient is curious enough to want to know the special discount price they'll click through to your customized sales page where your main sales copy should take over and do its job.*

STEP 14: ANNOUNCE YOUR BOOK/EBOOK

After your website is up and running you'll want to spread the word about its existence as quickly and widely as possible to attract visitors.

It's important to remember that the number of sales you make will be a direct function of the number of <u>targeted</u> visitors who come to your site.

Get Indexed In the Free Search Engines

By "targeted" visitors I am referring to those people searching online for info <u>directly related</u> to your product or service, and therefore most likely to be using your most important keyword words/phrases. (See page 57).

A lot of things have occurred in the online search engine (SE) world since I published the first edition of this book back in 2004.

The Big Three Free SEs

The most important thing that has happened in recent years is that there has been a shake-out in the SE industry and there are now only three major SE players: google.com, yahoo.com, and msn.com.

Google.com is by far the largest SE; handling more than 65 % of all search traffic. Yahoo.com now accounts for about 20% of traffic, and msn.com plus the many other smaller SEs handle the other 15% of searches.

The second important change is that the Big Three SEs (i.e. google, yahoo, msn) are now all very pro-active in seeking out new content as soon as it becomes available online and adding it to their indexes as quickly as possible. The challenge for the major SEs these days is to be the first to list the highest quality and freshest content for each subject for which people are searching for online.

So, getting your site properly indexed in the Big Three SEs is the most critical step if you want to get no-cost targeted visitors coming to your new website.

Up until a couple of years ago this was a somewhat complicated and often costly process that involved the once "secret and mysterious black art" of Search Engine Optimization (SEO).

Now, getting your pages indexed in the major SEs is a much simpler, less mysterious, and less expensive process. In fact, as long as your pages use standard html and meta tag protocols your new pages will likely get indexed by the Big Three SEs within a week or two of being uploaded; often in a matter of a few days.

Nevertheless, just to be sure, the first time I upload one of my mini-sites I still use a search engine submission service to publicize my site to as many free SEs as possible, including the hundreds of small ones beyond the Big Three. Collectively, these smaller SEs can still account for a significant amount of traffic, so it is worth some extra effort and expense to get listed in them.

A few years ago someone recommended an Australia-based SE submission service that I've been very happy with ever since. It's called ineedhits.com.
http://www.ineedhits.com

Ineedhits offers a basic SE submission service that will submit your URL to over 300 search engines (including google) for a mere $2.99. Now that's hard to beat.

That company offers a variety of other SE submission packages. It also offers what are known as "search engine optimization services" (SEO) that are supposed to help your website rank higher at the SEs. As I said above, placement in the SEs is much less dependent on SEO techniques than it used to be, so use such SEO services at your own discretion.

Personally, I have never used the SEO part of that service and I've always managed to get pretty good rankings at the major SEs. I just make sure I keep current on the SEO subject in general, and adjust my pages and meta tags from time-to-time.

Just to be sure you're covered on this, ask whoever designed and HTML-coded your site if they included proper "meta tags" in your website pages. If they answer affirmatively, great! If they don't seem to know what you're talking about, get ineedhits or another SEO expert to verify the SE-friendliness of your site.

Use Paid SEs To Advertise Your Site

In addition to the listings in the free search engine directories as discussed above, there are two other primary ways to get your site listed among the search results at those search engines; however these are not free.

First, are pay-per-inclusion services (PPI). These allow you to pay some search engines to include your site URL in their overall directory so that your site will show up somewhere in their search results.

Second, are pay-per-click advertising services (PPC). With these you can advertise by placing your ads in an SE's advertising distribution network and only pay when someone clicks on your ad link which will take them to your preferred destination website. This is called pay-per-click advertising.

Pay-Per-Inclusion Search Engines

A pay-per-inclusion search engine service is one where a webmaster pays a fee for guaranteed inclusion in the index of a search engine. There is normally a fixed fee charge for each unique URL that one wants included in an SE's index and network.

A few years ago there were a number of major/medium SEs offering pay-per-inclusion services. Now, the only significant such service is the paid submission service offered by Yahoo!

With the Yahoo! service you can buy guaranteed inclusion of your website(s) in the Yahoo! index for $49/yr., per URL. This guarantees inclusion of your site in Yahoo!'s main directory, which feeds its network. It does not however guarantee that your site will receive a high ranking.

The Yahoo! network includes some former major SE players including, altavista.com, excite.com, all theweb.com, and fast.com.
http://www.ineedhits.com/paid-inclusion/yahoo-search-submit-basic.aspx

Bottom line: SE pay per inclusion is not a big factor anymore. However, for only $49 per year I would still consider paying for guaranteed inclusion of a single URL in the Yahoo! Network, since it is still a major player.

I should mention that ineedhits offers a pseudo pay-per-inclusion service which guarantees that your small keyword based ad will get Top 10 exposure across 250 of the smaller SEs. You can check that product out at the following link:
http://www.ineedhits.com/pay-per-click/top-up-traffic.aspx

Pay-Per-Click Search Engines

At pay-per-click (PPC) search engines you pay a clickthrough charge every time someone clicks on one of your links that is included in an advertisement. That link redirects the person doing the clicking to your website.

The big attraction of PPC advertising is that you can set up your campaigns in a matter of minutes and within an hour or less have PPC traffic coming to your website. Not only does this have instant gratification benefits, but it is also a great way to quickly and easily test and fine-tune your advertising campaigns.

However, this is NOT free traffic; so one has to be careful while testing, or PPC advertising can quickly get very expensive.

Most pay-per-click networks offer competitive bidding systems that allow you to bid for a ranking position for a particular keyword and/or phrase. For example, if you bid $0.12 for the keyword phrase "business letter" at a PPC, that bid may give you second place, just behind someone else's first place bid of $0.14 for that term.

This means that whenever someone on that PPC's network enters the exact phrase "business letter" your listing will be displayed in second place in the search results that user receives from the SE. Because you have bid $0.12 for that placement, each time a searcher clicks on your listing you will be charged $0.12.

The big advantage of pay-per-click search engines is that you can bid on your top keywords/phrases and have highly targeted traffic coming to your website in literally minutes or hours. No search engine optimization tactics are required.

Originally, pay-per-click services were offered exclusively by search engines that were dedicated to providing pay-per-click services only. The largest of these was an SE called overture.com (formerly goto.com). However, in recent years The Big Three SE's have all gotten into the PPC business in a serious way.

The largest PPC is Google's PPC service called AdWords. Yahoo! bought overture.com a few years ago and now calls its PPC service Yahoo! Search Marketing, and MSN's PPC service is called MSN AdCenter.

In addition to the PPC services offered by the Big Three, there are still a few smaller dedicated PPC services operating such as MIVA, Enhance, 7Search, SearchFeed, ABCSearch, among others.

http://www.miva.com
http://www.enhance.com
http://www.7search.com

Google AdWords

Because Google AdWords is currently the leader in PPC advertising programs in terms of volume of traffic, quality of search results, and sophistication of user interface, I will briefly summarize how it works below.

Although Google is primarily known as a universal free search engine, it also offers the most important and successful pay-per-click advertising model called AdWords.

This program is different from the traditional PPCs in the sense that you don't engage in bidding directly against your competitors for keywords/phrase listings. Instead, the AdWords program displays small text ads on the right-hand side of the Google search results page for specific generic keyword searches. Advertisers who sponsor and create these ads pay a pre-specified maximum amount each time someone clicks on their particular Google Adwords ad.

To see Google AdWords in action go to www.google.com and perform a keyword search for the example we've been using, "furniture design".

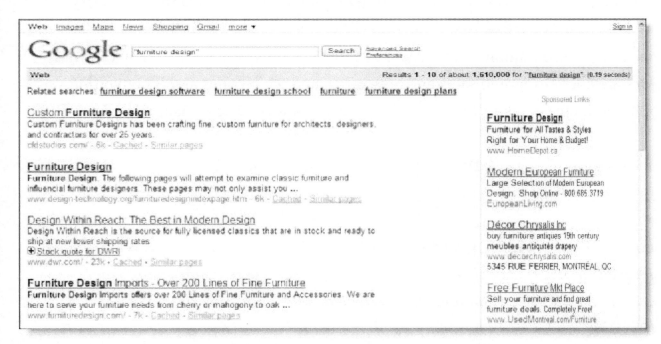

The search results shown on the left-hand side above are normal organic results.

The four ads on the right-hand side of the screen shot are Google AdWords ads. Advertisers will pay google a fee every time a searcher clicks on any of those links. If you were one of those advertisers that visitor would be directed to your website.

Google pioneered "intelligent content advertising" technology which ensures that your ads will only be displayed on websites/pages with content (and visitors) directly related to your chosen keywords.

One of the features that is so attractive about Google AdWords is that within a matter of minutes you can register and have an AdWords campaign up and running. Whenever you make changes to your campaign settings you will normally see the actual results of your changes reflected within a few minutes. It's almost real-time.

The feature that I really like about AdWords is that it gives you a breakdown of the effectiveness (or ineffectiveness) of your campaign on a keyword-by-keyword basis. It also offers a variety of analytical tools and capabilities so that you can optimize your campaigns to ensure you are maximizing your conversion potential. (ROI).

This kind of information is invaluable of course. It tells you exactly what keyword clicks are converting into sales and how often, and which ones aren't converting. So, it eliminates much of the guesswork and saves wasted advertising dollars.

To sign-up for Google AdWords go to the following link:

https://adwords.google.com/select/Login

Google AdSense Tip: *While you're at the Google website you will probably notice references to a service called Google AdSense which might confuse you. Don't worry about AdSense right now. With a typical sales-mini-site, the AdSense advertising model won't normally be of interest to you. It is mostly designed for information and/or content-oriented websites that have lots of blank space and don't* *mind visitors clicking away from their pages to an advertiser's page. Of course, with a sales-mini-site focused on your book/ebook, the last thing you want is for people to be clicking away to other sites, especially those of your competition.*

You can check out the PPC advertising services of the other two members of the Big Three at the following links:

Yahoo! Search Marketing

http://searchmarketing.yahoo.com/as/

MSN Digital Content Advertising

http://advertising.microsoft.com/home/home

For a comprehensive rundown on pay-per-click search engines and everything that one needs to know about PPC advertising, visit the following excellent website: http://www.payperclicksearchengines.com/

WARNING: Whenever you run a pay-per-click campaign at any PPC service you have to be careful to closely monitor your campaigns and set limits on them to make sure your advertising spending doesn't spiral out of control. All of the major PPC services provide you with tools to help you monitor your campaigns.

Issue A News Release

A news release, or press release, is what you need to issue to tell the world at large about your new book/ebook. If you haven't done one before, don't worry about it. Writing a news release for a specific product is not difficult.

In fact, you should be able to draft one yourself using any one of the eight news releases I have issued over the past few years:
http://writinghelptools.com/news.html

If you're reluctant to write your own press release, go to www.google.com and enter the phrase "write press release". There you will find links to dozens of "how-to" articles and websites, as well as many services which will write one for a fee.

The distribution service I have found to be excellent is PRWeb.com - The Free Wire Service. Registration is free. Here's their info and sign-up page:
http://www.prweb.com/sharenews.php

That service has a simple copy-and-paste user interface and they can have your news release issued to their extensive distribution network within 24 to 48 hours, or at a later date that you can specify.

Although the basic news release service at PRWeb.com is free, I normally upgrade by $20 or more to get a higher ranking on the date of my release.

Every month my sites receive hundreds of targeted clickthroughs from my PRWeb releases. That service also provides excellent activity statistics.

For many possible alternatives to PRWeb go to www.google.com and enter "distribute press release".

STEP 15: MARKET YOUR BOOK/EBOOK

In addition to the initial launch and announcement activities covered in the previous two steps, there are a number of other actions that you can take to publicize and promote your book/ebook. Generally speaking, these are known as "marketing" activities.

Below, I will summarize the main marketing activities that have worked for me.

Writing Articles

Sometimes called "article marketing", this is an excellent strategy. You simply write short articles related to the theme of your book/ebook and submit them to newsletter editors, webmasters and free content lists/sites, of which there are hundreds.

In the past couple of years I've published 35 to 40 articles related to the "writing help" theme of my websites and ebooks. Those articles have been picked up by hundreds of newsletter editors, blogs and websites all over the Net. Each month they drive hundreds of targeted visitors to my websites.

You can take a look here at some of my writing help related articles:
http://www.writinghelp-central.com/articles.html

The reason that the article writing/submission strategy works so well is that webmasters and/or newsletter and blog editors are always looking for free content to keep their websites and/or newsletters and blogs current and fresh.

It is universally understood by all parties online that, in exchange for using your free article content, a brief "resource box" at the end of your article will contain a short blurb about the author as well as a "live" hyperlink back to your website. (see the "publishing guidelines" statement posted at the articles link above).

There are literally hundreds of thousands of newsletters and blogs, and millions of websites, so chances are good that there are quite a few with a direct or indirect interest in your theme. These are the ones that will want to publish your material.

The primary way that webmasters find articles to post on their websites and blogs is by visiting "article directory sites" and searching for articles related to their theme. There are literally hundreds and hundreds of article directories where you can post your articles so that webmasters and bloggers will be able to select them. One of the most popular and respected is ezinearticles.com:

http://ezinearticles.com/

A few years ago I purchased Michael Southon's excellent ebook "Ezine Writer" which told me everything I needed to do to get my articles published online. That ebook was exactly what I needed at the time to get started and I still use most of the strategies I learned from that eBook.

However, I just noticed that Michael has since transferred the URL for that ebook over to a chap called Chris Knight who has extended the basic ebook into a comprehensive "Article Production Strategies" workshop which includes various audio tapes and related documents for a very reasonable price:

http://shop.ezinearticles.com/articleproduction/

Once you have written a few articles and started posting them to directories it can become a very laborious and time-consuming process. The article submission process at each directory is basically a manual one and you may find that you want to post each article to many directories for maximum exposure. Fortunately, article submission software has been developed to automate the process. Here's what I use:

http://articlesubmitterpro.com/

For more information on this go to www.google.com and enter "ezine publishing".

Joint Ventures

A simple online joint venture is when two webmasters join forces to promote the product of one and/or the other, or both. It's almost always a win-win situation.

A typical example occurred with me a couple of years ago when I did a small joint venture with Rosalind Gardner. Ros and I were exchanging e-mails on typical webmaster stuff one day when we discovered that our e-mail subscriber lists were almost identical in size.

So, Rosalind suggested that we "exchange lists" because she felt that one or more of my writing help ebooks would be of interest to her subscribers.

I thought that was a great idea, se we quickly agreed to do a joint-venture. I was pretty sure that many of my subscribers would be interested in Rosalind's "rags to riches" story, and that some of them might well be interested in purchasing Rosalind's *Super Affiliate Handbook*.

Here's the e-mail that I sent to my newsletter subscribers about Rosalind's product:

> Hello Robert,
>
> No, this isn't the Writing Help Update newsletter!
>
> Sorry, I'll be sending that to you in about 10 days or so. I just wanted to share some info with you since you're one of my Course graduates and/or newsletter subscribers.
>
> As you know, it's rare that I ever promote someone else's product. But, this time I've decided to make an exception.
>
> That's because it's actually a writing-related success story that I'd like to share with you - about how a friend of mine, has penned her own best-selling eBook. Here's the story...
>
> Some months ago I was contacted by Rosalind Gardner to help her finalize her new eBook just before she launched it.
>
> At the time, Ros needed a second pair of eyes to do a final editorial review and challenge before the final release. Her eBook is titled:

"The Super Affiliate Handbook: How I Made $436,797 Last Year Selling Other Peoples' Stuff Online". (Impressive title I thought, but was it for real?).

Rosalind sent me her draft and I went to work on it doing my editorial review. The draft was very well written, but I still I ended up spending well over 20 hours on the final fine-tuning.

Well I have to tell you, I was extremely impressed by the content of Rosalind's book. She had packed it with solid, no-nonsense, step-by-step information on how just about anyone willing to make the effort can earn an excellent income through affiliate programs.

Have you seen all the online hucksters' hype about 'How to earn HUGE money on the 'Net'?

It's sickening! Most of them have never earned a dime online! They're trying to sell you some gimmick, or 'Internet Mall' that won't bring you 2 red cents. If you're tired of the B.S. and are ready to learn the truth about Internet and Affiliate marketing – stick around.

Reading Rosalind's story could change your life!
http://writinghelptools.com/cgi-bin/a/t.cgi?rg

In 1998, she was working as an air traffic controller. The ridiculous shifts were taking a huge toll on her health and happiness.

(Small world! It turns out that Rosalind and I had both worked for the same government department at one time).

Ros knew that she had to do something, and fast, or she was going to an early grave. And DO something, she did! By 2000, she had QUIT that job! ..because... she was making $10,000 per month from the Internet!

And last year she earned more than $430,000 online! What's even MORE amazing is that she did it without any previous business experience.

How did she do it?

All with Affiliate Programs - associations with online merchants such as Dell, Sony and eBay, and they want people just like you, me and Rosalind to sell their products.

Best of all, there is no easier or cheaper online business to start and operate. As an affiliate marketer, you never have to worry about:

* Development or production costs.
* Stocking inventory.
* Order or refund processing.
* Shipping.
* Ongoing customer service.

No other business allows that type of freedom. And it gets better. Because you're working 'online' you can live where you please and work when you want.

For Rosalind, it's been a dream come true - and you can have it too!

Read her best-selling step-by-step guide, "The Super Affiliate Handbook: How I Made $436,797 Last Year Selling Other Peoples' Stuff Online", to learn exactly how she does it.

Better yet, Rosalind is offering her ebook to you, as a Writing Help Update subscriber, for the best price available anywhere online!

Simply click the link below and start now!
http://writinghelptools.com/cgi-bin/a/t.cgi?rg

All the best,
Shaun Fawcett
P.S.
Don't wait! You too can enjoy the lifestyle and freedom that Rosalind and others have discovered by operating an affiliate marketing business. Why work your butt off for an unappreciative boss, for small returns, when your own Internet business can give you all the money you'll ever need? Simply click the link below and start now!
http://writinghelptools.com/cgi-bin/a/t.cgi?rg

Rosalind supplied me with most of the above copy and then I combined it with some of my own material to create something suitable for my newsletter readers. Rosalind then sent the following e-mail to her people telling them all about me and my products with links to my websites.

Hello Christine,

If the cold weather isn't a great clue that it's winter in the Northern hemisphere, then the massive amounts of good stuff happening online should tell you that many folks are spending lots of time in front of their computers programming and writing.

It's VERY cool to see, and it's keeping me very busy both reading all the new info, checking out new software, and writing my thoughts about it all.

It also made me think again what a shame it is that writing is one thing that stops many folks from even trying to start an Internet business.

Do YOU struggle to put the right words onto a blank piece of paper or an empty screen?

If you do, you definitely aren't alone! In fact, it's estimated that at least 80% of us suffer from "writer's block" at some point in time. Many suffer from it on a regular basis.

Enter my online buddy Shaun Fawcett.

He helped me greatly with the Super Affiliate Handbook, and did all the editorial work.

Shaun is also the Webmaster of a number of popular "writing help" Web sites as well as the author of a number of ebooks on that same subject. His ebooks are specifically designed to help people overcome writer's block when doing a variety of different kinds of day-to-day practical writing.

His ebooks cover everything from writing personal and business letters, and resumes, to how to write letters of recommendation and reference letters, as well as resignation letters. He even has a book out on how to write college admission essays!

As far as I know, Shaun is the foremost online expert when it comes to producing "writing help" ebooks.

I first met Shaun online a little over a year ago. At the time I was suffering from a severe personal case of writer's block. Shaun soon sent me an article he had written called "Secrets For Beating Writer's Block". I was truly amazed by what that one piece of advice taught me about how to get over writer's block. Using a couple of his suggestions, in no time at all the words were flowing again.

Thankfully, since I started following Shaun's advice, I haven't had to deal with that dreaded condition again.

BUT, Shaun's real claim to fame are his fully-formatted "real-life templates". That's why every one of his writing help toolkits involves a two-pronged approach:

THE FIRST PART of each Kit is a comprehensive eBook full of tips, tricks, pointers, information and samples that tell you everything you need to know about writing a particular kind of letter or other document. A mini-"how to" style guide, if you like.

THE SECOND PART of each of Shaun's Writing Kits (and this is the kicker!) is a COMPLETE SET of ALL of the fully-formatted real-life samples from the "how to" part of the Kit that you can download directly into your word processing program and work with as you please!

That's right, you just download Shaun's MS-Word file packed with complete pre-written fully-formatted letters into your word processor and just start cutting, copying and pasting. It's as easy as child's play.

Working with these templates you'll have your own customized professional quality letter in a matter of a few minutes. The way I see it, that's a powerful way to beat writer's block anytime!

So, if you're looking for help with day-to-day PERSONAL writing tasks including letters, resumes, reports and/or essays, including over 60 real-life downloadable templates, you must check out Shaun's Instant Home Writing Kit:
http://hop.clickbank.net/hop.cgi?webvista2/instantkit

Or, if you're a BUSINESS person who could use a complete style guide on writing business letters, including over 100 real-life letters, forms and templates, I strongly suggest you take a look at Instant Business Letter Kit:
http://hop.clickbank.net/hop.cgi?webvista2/busletkit

All the best,

Rosalind
P.S. If Shaun's writing kits don't get you over writer's block the only other thing I might suggest is a "shrink", and you know how much they cost! :-)) Try Shaun's remedy first:

Instant Home Writing Kit:
http://hop.clickbank.net/hop.cgi?webvista2/instantkit

InstantBusinessLetterKit:
http://hop.clickbank.net/hop.cgi?webvista2/busletkit

When all was said and done, Rosalind and I split the proceeds from sales of our respective products. Hence the term "joint venture". There are literally scores of different types of joint venture arrangements that webmasters can make. Essentially, it's whatever makes sense, and whatever the two parties agree to.

If you produce a quality product, word will get around, and webmasters in your niche will begin approaching you, suggesting joint ventures.

On the other hand, if you have a quality product you don't need to be shy about approaching other webmasters in your niche. Just make sure that they also have a product that is appropriate for you to promote to your own subscribers.

For more information and resources on joint ventures go to www.google.com and enter the term "online joint ventures".

Affiliate Referrals

What I'm talking about here is the situation whereby other webmasters refer targeted visitors from their site to yours, using specially coded affiliate links that can be tracked by affiliate tracking software.

Say for example, you have written an ebook all about designing and building furniture for the home handyman. There will no doubt be numerous webmasters with related sites that would be interested in referring their visitors to your website to take a look at your book. A site that sells woodworking tools for example; or a woodworking hobby site might be another.

Chances are that some of these webmasters would be interested in recommending a book about home furniture design and assembly to their visitors – especially if they get a good commission when a sale is made!

That's how it works. If one of those referred visitors purchases your book/ebook while at your site, the webmaster that referred them to your site will then receive a pre-agreed commission, and you as the owner of the product site, get to keep the balance of a sale that you otherwise would not have made.

Typically, affiliate commissions for ebooks range between 30% and 50%.

From a merchant's perspective, the easiest way to do this is via ClickBank; since it has a built-in affiliate tracking and commission payment system. (See pg 95).

So, if you're a ClickBank merchant, the only thing you're prospective affiliates need to do is simply sign-up for free at ClickBank to get their own affiliate "nickname".

To see how this works, you can take a look at one of my affiliate sign-up pages here: http://www.instantbusinessletterkit.com/affiliates.html

Scroll to the bottom of that page and then click on the link labeled as follows:

> ### Click Here To Sign-Up With ClickBank
> It's easy, fast and free!

Clicking on that link will display the following message from ClickBank:

Affiliate Program: Promote Products

You can earn 40% for each paying customer you refer to this product. For details please enter your ClickBank nickname

ClickBank NickName: [   ]

Tracking ID (Optional): [   ]

[Create]

No nickname? Click HERE to sign up first. Its free!

Once your prospective affiliate has entered their "nickname" (in this example "xxxxxxxx"), the following box will give them their ClickBank affiliate links:

Affiliate Program: Promote Products

ClickBank pays you 40% when you sell this publishers product. To refer a customer send them to this domain name:

http://xxxxxxxx.busletkit.hop.clickbank.net/

Cut and paste the following hoplink into your web page:

<a href="http://xxxxxxxx.busletkit.hop.clickbank.net/" target="_top">Click Here!</a>

All your affiliate partner has to do is place one or more of these ClickBank affiliate "hoplinks" on their website with the "xxxxxxxx" nickname replaced with their own ClickBank nickname. Now, anyone who clicks on that hoplink will be taken directly to your product website where you try to convert them into a sale.

The specially coded hoplink allows ClickBank's affiliate auto-tracking software to keep track of that referral when they arrive at your website and determines whether they make a purchase or not.

If the referral does make a purchase while at your website, the referring webmaster will automatically receive commissions in their ClickBank account on any sale made to the person who clicked through to the product site via that hoplink.

The above is just one example of how this affiliate referral and commission process works; using ClickBank as an example.

As a merchant selling your book/ebook there are dozens of other affiliate networks you can join other than ClickBank if you'd like.

For detailed information on affiliate networks and many other affiliate/associate program issues, I suggest you go to Al Gardyne's extensive website on this subject: http://www.associateprograms.com/

This affiliate referral strategy works best when you have set up a general content site that contains info all about your particular niche.

As I mentioned earlier, it is NOT a good idea to place affiliate links to the sites of other people's products directly on your own product's a sales-mini-site because it will distract visitors from focusing on your product.

For example, I have many strategically-placed affiliate referral links on my high traffic free content site; Writing Help Central: http://www.writinghelp-central.com

However, I have been careful not to place affiliate links on web pages where they would be in direct competition with a link to one of my sales-mini-sites.

Ezine Advertising

I have tried Ezine advertising on and off for a few years with mixed results. It's a strategy that many of the so-called Internet marketing gurus swear by.

There are apparently over 400,000+ ezines being published online these days. No doubt, some of these ezines that operate in your particular niche have subscribers that might be interested in your book/ebook.

The basic idea with this method is for you to find those ezines with readers that best fit your target audience and then advertise in some of those ezines.

Ezine advertising has two big drawing cards: 1) an ezine that matches your theme or niche will have highly targeted subscribers for your ads, and 2) ezine advertising can be relatively inexpensive.

The main reason why I'm not doing much ezine advertising these days is because of the situation with the proliferation of spam online and the resulting spam filters.

My reasoning being: what's the point of paying for advertising in an ezine with a circulation of 15,000 subscribers when, quite possibly, only about 10% to 20% of the e-mails are getting through the spam filters?

Until the spam situation improves I don't think I'll be doing much ezine advertising.

Nevertheless, if you want to give it a shot, either now or when the situation improves, there is a great service that will help you quickly find ezines that target your potential buyers.

It's run by Charlie Page and it's called Directory of Ezines:
http://www.directoryofezines.com

Offer A Free Mini-Course

One of the most successful marketing methods I've come across is to offer a free mini-course directly related to my site theme, to all of my site visitors.

As visitors leave my site they see the following pop-under form offering the Course:

Since most of my websites are writing help related, I am able to use this particular pop-under on a number of my websites.

I often use a pop-"under" rather than a pop-"up" because they are less annoying. Pop-unders appear only as the visitor is leaving the site, rather than interfering with their visit as pop-ups tend to do.

This technique yields me over 300 highly targeted sign-ups each and every week. Notice how prospects get to opt-in for both my Course and my Blog with the same sign-up.

Including a welcome message and a couple of post-course follow-ups, my Course autoresponder series consists of 10 e-mails delivered over a three-week period. If you haven't taken it yet you can sign up right here to see how it works:

http://instanthomewritingkit.com/free-course.html

Offering such a Course is a powerful way to build trust and credibility with your subscribers. It also gives you an excellent chance to introduce them to all of your products and to do "soft" up-sells.

Make sure you offer quality information that your subscribers will find useful. For them, the quality of the Course will be their number one indicator as to the probable level of quality of the products you are selling.

You are welcome to sign up for any or all of the five courses that I currently offer at: http://www.writinghelptools.com/all-courses.html

Publish A Regular Newsletter

As mentioned above, online newsletters are commonly referred to as ezines.

For the first few years that I was online I published a monthly "writing help" newsletter that I sent to all people who had "opted-in" to receive one or more of my free courses. (In recent years I have replaced that newsletter with a blog; a strategy I will explain in the next section).

Some webmasters publish more frequently, even weekly, but for me that would be too distracting and too much work. Also, I think the limit that my subscribers would find acceptable is twice a month, maximum.

To give you an idea of what I am talking about, the following link will take you to see a typical edition of what my online ezine or newsletter looked like just before I switched to my current blog strategy: http://writinghelptools.com/WHMMar0105.html

Offering Course subscribers a content-based newsletter or ezine is an excellent way to continue to nurture their trust and loyalty after they have completed the Course.

Using this method, in just a few years I have been able to build a 100% opt-in list of more than 30,000 loyal subscribers.

Again, it's important to make sure you are providing quality information on a regular basis. It's a great way to promote your products as long as you're subtle about it. You can promote other products too, as long as they're theme-related.

Typically, newsletters are sent as e-mails, either in text, or formatted in html. The last year or so that I published my newsletter I posted it online in html format (See link to the example on the previous page). I would then send a short announcement e-mail advising people that the newsletter was now available to read online.

I did it this way for two reasons. One; the short announcement e-mail with only one hyperlink was more likely to get through the spam filters than a lengthy e-mail containing all kinds of links. Two; I found that it was easier to set-up and format my newsletter online in html.

Also, there didn't seem to be any downside as far as my subscribers were concerned. In fact, it was easier for them to read the online version than the e-mail edition.

No matter how you do it, sending a regular update (i.e. ezine, newsletter, blog post) to your subscribers is a must if you want to keep the relationship going.

For information on creating a newsletter, the "how-to guru" Michael Green has developed a great product -- *How To Write A Newsletter Toolkit*. Here's the link: http://www.howtowriteanewsletter.com/

If you buy that Toolkit from here, Michael will upgrade you to one of his premium levels. Just e-mail him after your purchase at: mailto:michael@howtocorp.com and state in your e-mail: "Shaun Fawcett HTWAN Upgrade Special Please Michael".

Attracting Additional Targeted Traffic

Over the last few years I have tried a lot of different ways to get highly targeted traffic to my websites. I've used conventional approaches including: free search engines and directories, pay-per-inclusion services, pay-per-click services, writing and posting articles, and others; all of which I've discussed earlier. (See page 106).

In addition, I have also developed a couple of my own exclusive targeted traffic generators that work very nicely. I didn't get these specific techniques from any of the "gurus" either. They just sort of evolved as my ebooks and websites evolved.

Use "Back Door" Pages

This strategy involves developing some legitimate "content" pages linked to your sales-mini-site. Targeted traffic will arrive at those pages from the search engines to view that content and then some of your "strategically-placed links" on that page will direct some of those visitors to your sales-mini-site. The best way to explain this is with a couple of examples, as follows:

My Business Letter Kit site has links to three sample business letters.
http://instantbusinessletterkit.com

To see those sample letters, go to that website and scroll down about 60% of the page until you see the following headline:

Real-Life Templates Create Value-Added Richness

Just below that, you'll see three bulleted paragraphs with links to sample letters:
http://www.instantbusinessletterkit.com/rltemplate1.html (termination letter)
http://www.instantbusinessletterkit.com/rltemplate2.html (sales letter)
http://www.instantbusinessletterkit.com/rltemplate3.html (apology letter)

Take a look at those sample templates. You'll see that they are dual-purpose pages.

First, they provide additional information about your product to the visitors on your sales-mini-site and give them an example of the quality of your work.

Second, these pages are "out-there" on the Internet being indexed by the search engine crawlers as quality content pages to which targeted visitors will be sent.

So in this case, I get highly targeted visitors coming in the "back door" to my sales-mini-site because they are searching for sample letter templates for "termination letters", or "sales letters" or "apology letters". Many searchers click through from those templates to my sales-mini-site. Some buy my products.

Naturally, I chose these particular letter types because I know that they are three of the most searched for business letters on the Internet.

Believe me, I get hundreds of free and highly targeted visitors to my sales-mini-sites every month this way. If you check out my other websites, you'll see that I use different variations of this "back door page" method on each of my sales-mini-sites.

Create A Media Kit

This is another effective method for getting free targeted traffic and for creating cross-traffic among your various sites if you have more than one related site.

You could say that this technique is a cross between the back door pages method just described above and the news release method discussed earlier.

A "media kit" is a standard tool used in the PR business and is a very legitimate and useful thing for you to include on your website. Like the back door pages, it is also dual purpose in nature.

First, it provides your site visitors with additional information about you, your product, and your business. In fact, it's a big credibility builder.

Second, it's an additional magnet for "back door" visitors, many of whom will go on to click through to any one of your websites that are listed there.

A typical media kit consists of four parts as follows:

1. **News Release** – Use the same news release that you submit to a press distribution service in Step 14. (See page 114).

2. **Facts Sheet** – I use a Features/Benefits Fact Sheet that summarizes the highlights of the ebook from the sales page.

3. **Author Biography** – A brief biography of the ebook author including links to any related Web sites.

4. **Suggested Questions** – A standard component of a media kit designed to help journalists conduct an author interview. Also, it suggests to non-media readers which questions they should be asking and what answers they should be seeking.

Here are the media kits for a few of my ebook sales-mini-sites:

http://instantcollegeadmissionessay.com/mediakit.html
http://instantbusinessletterkit.com/mediakit.html
http://instantrecommendationletterkit.com/mediakit.html

Take note that I place the links to these media kits just below the header/masthead on the upper right of each sales-mini-site.
These media kits draw lots of "back door" traffic to each site and create some interesting cross-traffic among my various sites since they provide a little mini-index of all of my ebook websites.

Other Marketing Strategies

In addition to the foregoing marketing options there are a number of other strategies which you can use to get the word out about your book/ebook and generate sales.

Pay-Per-Click and Pay-Per-Inclusion Campaigns

These two advertising methods are explained in detail in the previous Section under the heading "Get Registered in the Search Engines" (See page 106).

I continue to use whatever pay-per-inclusion services are still available. At a cost of $2 to $3 per month per URL I think they're likely worth the relatively small investment since they expose your URL to multiple search engines and indexes in which they otherwise wouldn't be listed.

Google Ads

Google Ads is also covered in some detail in the previous Section under the heading "Get Registered in the Search Engines" (See page 106).

Since the Google Ads service first came out a few years ago, Google has been constantly refining the usefulness of the product for advertisers. It is quite a powerful tool, and if implemented and monitored carefully it can pay excellent dividends per advertising dollar. (See page 108).

Networking

Make an effort to get to know webmasters in your niche or area of interest. Check out their websites and send e-mails complimenting something about their site and/or products to break the ice.

Spend some time in online forums related to your subject and make some posts.

These relationships can pay off in all sorts of ways, such as joint venture proposals.

STEP 16: TAKE YOUR EBOOK DIGITAL

I know that some readers have been waiting patiently just to read what's in this section of this ebook. I can understand why too.

The information contained in this single Step is guaranteed to add thousands of dollars annually to your bottom line sales! That's right -- if you implement what I suggest here you are likely to sell hundreds more ebooks in addition to those you sell from your websites.

Digital Fulfillment: Definition

It's important that you understand exactly what I'm talking about when I use the term "digital fulfillment", as opposed to "POD fulfillment" (See Step 17, page 143).

Digital fulfillment refers to when your ebook is delivered strictly in electronic form as a digital download product. Essentially the same as when your ebook gets downloaded from your website, except that, the digital fulfillment is provided by a digital download distribution company.

A typical example of digital fulfillment in action would be when you provide your ebook electronic files (PDF) to a company that distributes ebooks to amazon.com, for example. Amazon.com would then offer your ebook to its customers as a digital download product.

Discovering The Secret of Digital Fulfillment

As I stated in the Introduction I have spent the past few years immersing myself in learning about the tools and techniques of successful Internet marketing to help me sell more of my ebooks/books.

In the process, I have purchased dozens of "must have" books from many heavy-hitter big-name Internet marketers.

But NEVER have I read about this strategy that I'm going to share right now in ANY of those many books/ebooks from the Internet Marketing gurus!

In fact, the only way I stumbled across this largely unknown money-making secret was when I asked a simple and logical "what if" question. Here's what I innocently asked customer service at amazon.com one day a few years ago.

Hello at amazon.com,

I have had two regular paperback books listed on your site for some time now and they sell reasonably well. I have since developed a couple of digital download ebooks that are selling quite well from my Web sites. I was wondering what would be involved in getting these ebooks listed on amazon.com?
Thanks very much,

Shaun Fawcett

Here's the simple answer I received.

Dear Shaun,

Yes, we do list ebooks, but not via our Advantage Program through which your paperbacks are listed. You will have to get your ebooks listed with a publisher/distributor of digital download ebooks such as Lightning Source. Thanks for your inquiry,

Brad,
Customer Support
Amazon.com

I didn't realize it at the time, but that was a breakthrough moment for me.

So, I decided to check out this Lightning Source and here's what I found out:

Lightning Source Incorporated (LSI) is known as a digital fulfillment company. It claims to be the industry-leader in providing combined book manufacturing and distribution services. Powered by the world's leading digital book library, LSI stores books electronically and delivers them "on demand" as e-books, or as traditional printed books, in response to orders from publishers, booksellers, and librarians. http://www.lightningsource.com

That company is revolutionizing the options available to the publishing industry in the storage, management and distribution of digital content. As I write this, Lightning Source has printed more than 30,000,000 "on-demand" books for more than 4,300 publishers around the world.

When I read that Lightning Source was owned by Ingram Industries this got me really excited. That's because I knew from my days in the offline publishing world that Ingram was one of the major book distributors in the United States. Here's an excerpt from what they say on one of their Web sites:

Ingram Book Group is a leading wholesaler of trade books, spoken audio, and magazines. Through its OneSource partnerships, Ingram also distributes music, DVD, video, Spanish language, and medical reference titles, and used and out-of-print books. Ingram and its partners provide immediate delivery of over 1 million titles. Ingram's operating units include Ingram Book Company, Ingram Periodicals Inc., Ingram International Inc., Ingram Library Services Inc., Spring Arbor Distributors Inc., Tennessee Book Company, Ingram Fulfillment Services Inc. and Ingram Customers Systems Inc. For more information

Bottom line: it's a vast distribution network, folks. It means much more than just getting your ebook and/or book listed on amazon.com. It means getting your title in front of more than 80% of all book wholesalers and retailers!

Why Choose Digital Fulfillment?

The underlying question here being: If your books are available as ebooks via your websites AND in print via POD distributors, why go to the trouble of also offering them as digital download books through digital download channels?

That's a good logical question, and you may be surprised by the answer.

I have found that there is very little cross-over between the people that buy ebooks at my websites and those who buy them through sites like amazon.com.

In fact, out of thousands of sales through both channels I have only received one e-mail that indicated a buyer had seen my ebooks at both places.

Another proof of this is that although I use the same list price for my ebooks on my websites and at amazon.com, that company often chooses to offer a 30% discount, which makes it a much better deal to buy the ebook at their website.

In spite of this, sales at my websites remain strong. In fact I continue to sell more ebooks from my websites. So, it's pretty clear that people aren't doing cross-comparisons of prices. These appear to be mutually exclusive groups of shoppers.

I believe the main reason for this is due to the "vertical" nature of the Internet information search.

That is, when someone searches for specific info based on a keyword phrase they are first presented with a single screen full of results. So, regardless of how many actual "results" the search engine has found for that particular inquiry (often in the tens of thousands) the searcher sees 10 to 20 results on the first results page presented on their screen. Research has shown that the vast majority of people will click on one of the first few links on that first results page.

Once a searcher has clicked through from the SE's search results page to a specific info and/or product page, chances are that if what they find there is a good match with what they are looking for they will stay there and investigate it in detail. Some of those people will buy a product while there.

I have found that the form that the info is in (i.e., ebook, digital download, paper) is a secondary concern once people believe they have found the info that will help them solve their problem. Again, the "instant gratification" factor takes precedence.

The key point here being -- if I didn't offer my ebooks online through amazon.com and others I would probably not make over 95% of those sales through my other distribution channels (i.e. my websites). Ouch, that hurts!

I've noted something interesting about the mind-set of customers at amazon.com and those who arrive at my websites. As you know from reading this, a lot of thought and effort goes into developing a well-designed sales-mini-site. It takes up to 3,500 words of persuasive sales copy specifically written to convert that targeted visitor from a "browser" to a "buyer". If you're good (and/or lucky) you might be able to get 1 or 2 visitors out of every 200 – 250 to buy your product. Meanwhile, at amazon.com, shoppers find your ebook as the result of a keyword search and then all they see is the cover, a one paragraph write-up, and perhaps a couple of testimonials. Yet, the sale still gets made! So why do we have to work so much harder to make a sale on our websites as opposed to amazon.com? It's fairly obvious if you really think about it. The reason is this: the vast majority of visitors that arrive at your website have no intention to buy when they get there, and are generally looking for free information. On the other hand, the majority of shoppers at amazon.com have already decided before they even go there that they will make a purchase if they can find what they are looking for.

As stated above, I currently use LightningSource.com as my ebook digital fulfillment publisher/distributor. (See write-up on LightningSource.com above).

How Ebook Digital Fulfillment Works

Realizing how this digital fulfillment model works was a real eye-opener for me.

Here's the basic digital ebook fulfillment scenario for you...

1. You have produced your ebook in PDF format and you're already selling it from your website.

2. You decide you would like your ebook also to be available through online ebook retailers who sell digital download books.

3. You register online as a publisher with LightningSource.com or a similar ebook digital fulfillment company.

4. You fill out an online form to register your ebook title (for the past couple of years the normal $25 per title fee has been waived for ebooks at LSI).

5. You upload your ebook PDF file and a cover image via the LSI website.

That's it, you're in business! In 10 to 15 days or so you'll see your ebook showing up on websites that carry digital download ebooks.

The really exciting thing about these LSI-driven ebook sales is that they are IN ADDITION to any sales that you will make via your website.

As mentioned beore, there is virtually no cross-over between the two markets. So, this is almost like "found money". You just have to know how to find it.

Benefits Of Digital Fulfillment - Ebooks

Although I listed the benefits of the overall online publishing model in an earlier Section of this book titled "The Online Publishing Model", below is a summary of the benefits of publishing/distributing your ebook specifically through a digital fulfillment company such as LightningSource.com:

You Make Good Money

Even though you won't make quite as much money as you do selling straight from your website, you'll still make a lot more per sale via a digital fulfillment distributor than through the traditional book publishing model. For example, even though I have to discount my price by as much as 40% to get my ebook listed with companies like amazon.com, I still make 60% of my list price of $29.95. That's almost $18 per sale going directly to me! And, if the retailer decides to discount that price to their customers, that comes from their share of the sale, not mine.

Sales On Automatic Pilot

Once you've submitted your ebook PDF files and cover image to your digital fulfillment company you have nothing else to do. After that, their process kicks into action automatically. They look after all the marketing, publicity and distribution to book sellers. The next thing you'll know you'll be receiving regular monthly checks just for signing up.

Low Costs

There are virtually no out-of-pocket costs in getting your ebook listed online through a digital fulfillment distributor like LightningSource.com. Assuming that you've already produced your ebook and cover image for your website, the only possible additional cost to get listed online through a company like LSI is a possible registration fee for each new title. (As I mentioned above, at the time of this writing LSI was waiving their normal $25 fee for ebook title registrations).

No Returns Or Inventory

Unlike the traditional book publishing model, there is no forced allowance for "returns" because digital download ebooks are non-returnable when sold. In addition, by definition, there are no inventory management issues involved with digital fulfillment ebooks.

More Control and Flexibility

With digitally-fulfilled ebooks there is no tie-in to the 18-month publishing cycle of the traditional book publishing model. You can create and submit a new or revised ebook at any time and it will be posted online within a couple of weeks. The only constraint is that you will have to provide your fulfillment company with up to 90-days notice if you intend to change your price.

Instant Sales Information

Dealing with a digital fulfillment company like LightningSource.com, you'll have close to real-time online access to your sales and revenue statistics on a title-by-title basis. For example, I can sign-in to my LSI account online any time and find out my sales/revenue information up-to-date as of 48 hours previously.

Other Digital Fulfillment Companies

Throughout this section I have been talking about LightningSource.com as if it were the only digital fulfillment company for ebooks. Of course, it is not the only one, although I believe it is the biggest right now.

The reason I focus on LSI is because it's the one that I use and I've been very happy with their service to-date.

Also, as I pointed out above, because of LSI has corporate connections to Ingram Publishing, they offer access to a massive built-in distribution network, an advantage which should not be underestimated. (See page 135).

There are other digital fulfillment companies you can check out as well, such as:
http://www.iuniverse.com/ebook-publisher.htm

http://www.xlibris.com/

For other digital fulfillment distributors the section titled *Ebook Resources*, on page 159 of this book/ebook contains additional company listings.

Ebook Retailers

Because amazon.com is so predominant in the online book/ebook sales world I might have implied above that it is the only one worth being concerned with, which is not correct. There are a number of online ebook retailers that will promote and sell your ebook as a digital download.

For example, some of the eBook retailers that list my digital download eBooks are:

http://www.alibris.com/

http://www.ebookmall.com/

http://diesel-ebooks.com/

http://www.booksonboard.com/

All of my ebooks were automatically picked up by the above sites through my listings at lightningsource.com. I did nothing specific to get my ebook titles listed on those websites. So, make sure that whichever digital download distributor you use is networked with major ebook retailers such as those listed above.

For additional ebook retailers, check the section of this book titled *Ebook Resources*, on page 159 of this ebook contains additional company listings.

Recent Ebook Developments

Due to the constantly evolving nature of the Internet, changes are regularly taking place that will have varying degrees of impact on those doing business online. These changes are both technology-related and due to competitive forces that prevail in the marketplace.

A number of such factors have impacted the ebook world in recent years and will continue to do so in the foreseeable future. Following are a couple of significant developments that have taken place recently:

- The largest ebook retailer, amazon.com, has decided that in the future ebooks will be primarily read by people using handheld devices such as PDAs. Accordingly, that company has stopped supporting ebooks not formatted for those devices. (See page 45).

- As the largest player in the online book retailing marketplace (ebooks, paper books), amazon.com has decided to get into the publishing business so that it can compete directly with companies such as lightningsource.com and others.

The full impact of these events is far from clear as I write this. The only advice I can give you on this is to try to keep abreast of recent developments and adjust your strategies as required.

STEP 17: GO POD WITH YOUR EBOOK

As I was saying in the previous Step, I got pretty excited, when I found out about using the digital fulfillment model for ebooks.

However when I found out about how I could also take advantage of the print-on-demand (POD) model I was ecstatic!

POD Fulfillment: Definition

It's important that you understand exactly what I'm talking about when I use the term "POD fulfillment", as opposed to "digital fulfillment" (See Step 16).

POD fulfillment refers to when your book is delivered to the customer strictly in printed paper form as a standard book. With POD, when a single order (or low volume order) for your book is placed, just that small quantity is printed, bound and drop-shipped directly to the customer by your POD fulfillment company. Hence the term, print-on-demand.

A typical case of POD fulfillment in action would be when you provide your POD electronic files (PDF) to a company that distributes POD books to booksellers like amazon.com, for example. That book retailer would then offer your POD book to those of its customers who want a standard printed version of your book.

Why Choose POD Fulfillment?

When people order a print-on-demand book they get a real hard copy paperback book that they can hold in their hands.

But why choose to produce a POD version when you already offer an ebook version? This is a good and logical question.

The main answer is – an ebook is NOT a perfect substitute for a printed book.

This becomes particularly clear when marketing the two products through the same online bookseller. It turns out that even when the ebook version is offered at a 30% discount, about 40% of buyers who bought that very same title still choose the more expensive POD paperback version.

So, not only are these people willing to pay more, but they are also willing to wait anywhere from 3 to 5 days for the POD book to be delivered to them.

These are the traditional book buying people. They want a traditional book that they can hold in their hands. They want to be able to turn the pages. Many of these buyers don't really understand what an ebook or digital download is all about.

And, even if they do understand the "e" part of ebook they don't want to have anything to do with something that sounds so "techie".

Bottom line: *If you want to sell books to the traditional book buying public you have to give them an option that many people still want – a printed book. Print-on-demand (POD) let's you do just that -- one copy at a time.*

So, what does a POD book look like you might ask?

> *The quality of my POD books(LSI-produced) when printed is quite acceptable. The full-color glossy cover is printed on standard cover stock paper. The interior is comprised of standard 81/2" x 11" paper stock, printed both sides. It's like an excellent quality Xerox job between professionally designed full-color glossy covers. So, people who order them get a paperback of equivalent quality as to what one would normally find on the shelves at a bookstore.*

In fact, in my how-to book library I have a number of regular paperback "how-to" books that don't measure up to the level of quality of my LSI-produced POD books.

In summary, print-on-demand (POD) means exactly that. When someone wants a paperback copy of your book, they can order a single copy and the POD fulfillment company will print one copy only and drop-ship that copy directly to the buyer.

Once again, I use LightningSource.com as my POD fulfillment publisher/distributor. (See write-up on LightningSource.com in Step 16).

How POD Digital Fulfillment Works

Converting your ebook to a POD book involves a couple of extra steps, but overall it's relatively straightforward.

Here's the basic print-on-demand (POD) fulfillment scenario for you...

1. You have produced your ebook in PDF format and you're already selling it from your website, and possibly as a digital download through a digital fulfillment company (e.g. LSI).

2. You decide you would like your ebook to also be available as a paperback through standard book sellers everywhere including amazon.com, barnesandnoble.com, as well as thousands of offline book retailers.

3. You register online as a publisher with LightningSource.com or a similar POD fulfillment company.

4. You fill out an online form to register your POD title (Right now LSI charges a one-time set-up fee of $75 per title for POD books).

5. You upload your ebook PDF file and a cover images via the LSI Web site.

For a POD, point 5 above will involve some extra work and expense, as follows:

- If you don't have your cover art in 300 dpi you will need that. The publishing industry requires 300 dpi images for their marketing and publicity campaigns. As stated in Step 5, on ordering your ebook cover, if there's any chance that you might eventually go POD with your ebook, ask the cover designer to produce a 300 dpi image initially. This will save time and money later. (See page 72).

- In addition, for your POD you will need designs for a back cover and a spine and matching artwork in 300 dpi. This will be new, since there was no need for a back cover or spine for your ebook.

- You will also have to set-up and format your ebook PDF file slightly differently to accommodate the direct print-on-demand process for your POD book.

- In addition, you might want to add a couple of "Special Preface" pages into the POD edition of your book explaining how the original version is an ebook, how hyperlinks listed are not active, and whatever else is appropriate.

For example, in the POD version of my *Instant Recommendation Letter Kit,* I use the Special Preface to tell owners how they can send me an e-mail at a special address so that I can send them a copy by e-mail of the same letter templates file that online buyers normally download directly from my website.

Benefits Of POD Fulfillment – Printed Books

I listed the benefits of digital fulfillment for ebooks in Step 16 above. There are many similar benefits in providing print-on-demand printed books to your buyers:

You Make Good Money, But...

With your POD version you won't make quite as much money per sale as you will through ebook digital fulfillment because each time a POD book is printed, you the publisher, must pay for the cost of printing and shipping that book. But, you'll still make significantly more money per sale via POD than you would under the traditional book publishing model. For example, I pay $4.32 for each copy of my

170 page *Instant Recommendation Letter Kit* book, which means I still make about $14 per POD book, net of the printing cost. The print charge is a function of the number of pages, so it will increase as the length of your book increases.

Sales On Automatic Pilot

As with digital download ebooks, once you've submitted your POD PDF files and cover art work to your digital fulfillment company you have nothing else to do. After that, their process kicks into action automatically. They look after all the marketing, publicity and distribution to book sellers. Soon, you'll be receiving regular monthly checks just for signing up.

Lower Costs, But...

Again, there will be some additional costs with POD, but still a lot less than with the traditional book publishing model. You have to pay a title registration fee as well as printing fees for every copy ordered. In addition, as noted above, there will be a one-time charge for the extra artwork required for the back cover and spine.

No Returns Or Inventory

As with digital download ebooks, there is no forced allowance for "returns" because PODS are non-returnable when sold. In addition, by definition there are no inventory management issues involved with digital fulfillment POD books.

More Control and Flexibility

With POD books you will be able to produce a new version whenever it's ready. However, even though you won't be tied directly in to the 18-month publishing cycle of the traditional book publishing model, that cycle may affect your sales peaks and valleys. That's because many of your POD sales will be generated by the retail bookselling industry. You will also be required to give your POD fulfillment company up to 90-days notice if you intend to change your price.

Instant Sales Information

When you deal with a digital fulfillment company like LSI, you will have near real-time online access to your sales and revenue statistics. For example, I can sign-in to my LSI online account anytime and view my sales/revenue info to within 48 hours.

Other POD Fulfillment Companies

Throughout this section I have been talking about LightningSource.com as if it were the only digital fulfillment company for POD books, which it's not. I focus on LSI mainly because it's the one I use, and I've been happy with their service to-date.

For other digital fulfillment distributors the section titled *POD Resources*, on page *POD Resources*, on pages 159 of this ebook contains additional company listings.

Warning: Be careful not to get legitimate POD printers like LSI confused with the dreaded "vanity publishers", that often call themselves "POD publishers".
http://www.instantbookwritingkit.com/VanityPubs.html

A recent development worth mentioning is amazon.com's recent acquisition of BookSurge.com, a POD publisher that is in direct competition with Lightning Source.com. As I write this, claims are being made by some folks that amazon.com is soon going to force POD publishers to use BookSurge if they want their POD books listed for sale on the amazon.com website.
http://www.booksurge.com

Many folks in the online publishing world are upset about what they perceive as an unfair monopolistic practice by amazon. Although, I know that this has not happened yet because, as I write this, all of my POD titles are still listed at amazon.

This is a situation that we all need to watch carefully and adjust our plans and strategies as necessary.

CLOSING SUMMARY

As I stated in the Introduction, the primary purpose of this guide is to explain to readers exactly how I create, publish and market my own books/ebooks using online techniques and channels that deliberately sidestep the traditional book publishing model. The main reason for avoiding that conventional approach is that I consider it to be a highly dysfunctional business model that is not particularly helpful to the average small-time author and/or self-publisher. (See page 23).

Below are the main overall points that summarize what this book is all about.

KEY CONCLUSIONS

➤ There are many problems with the traditional book publishing model that work against the success of small time authors and/or self-publishers.

➤ With the advent of online Internet-based technology over the past decade, it is now possible for small-time authors and self-publishers to bypass the old model.

➤ The new Online Publishing Model (OPM), explained herein, offers many benefits to authors and publishers over the traditional publishing model.

➤ There is a series of very specific action steps and sub-steps (as detailed herein) that can be taken to successfully implement the Online Publishing Model.

In summary; the emergence of the Internet and related technologies has leveled the playing field for small-time authors and/or self publishers, allowing them to successfully create, publish and market their books/ebooks independent of the conventional publishing industry.

IMPLEMENTATION TOOLS AND RESOURCES

Before and during the implementation of the foregoing 17 Action Steps there are a number of issues that you will need to be aware of, as well as some tools and resources that will be helpful in producing your book/ebook.

The following sections cover the main implementation issues, tools and resources:

WHAT IT WILL COST YOU

This table contains an estimate of the approximate direct (out-of-pocket) costs that you will likely incur in implementing the previous 17 Steps for one book/ebook title.

COST ITEM	PAGE REF.	COST RANGE (US$)	
Register copyright (1 title)	61	$0	$50
Obtain ISBN (1 title)	62	$0	$55+
Register domain name (1 yr.)	64	$5	$10+
Cover/Website art work	67	$75	$125+
PDF creation	86	$0	$100+
Web site hosting (1 yr.)	92	$75	$100+
Write sales letter	93	$0	$1,000+
Payment processor account	95	$0	$50
Web site design/creation	98	$0	$1,000+
Initial SE submissions (free SEs)	106	$5	$10+
Initial pay-per-inclusion (1 yr)	106	$50	$50
Issue news/press release	113	$0	$20+
Digital fulfillment – 1 eBook	133	$0	$25
POD – 1 title	143	$75	$75
POD – artwork (back cover, spine)	145	$100	$150
Total Estimated Costs		**$380**	**$2,810+**

Costing Assumptions:

- Assumes the writing, publishing and initial marketing of one title using: a dedicated website (ebook), a digital fulfillment distributor (digital download/ebook), and a POD fulfillment distributor (POD book).

- The lower end of cost range (i.e. left-hand cost column) assumes that if it's something you can do for yourself, you do that, thus incurring no extra out-of-pocket costs (i.e. $0). Otherwise, the cost shown is the lowest cost service.

- The higher end of the cost range (i.e. right-hand cost column) displays what I consider to be a reasonable cost should you not be doing the tasks yourself or choosing the lowest possible price. The plus signs (+) indicate that there are other options available at a higher price, should you decide to use them.

The bottom-line is this: for one title, it will cost you somewhere between $380 and $2,810 to implement the 17 Action Steps covered earlier.

Let's put that in book sale terms that you can relate to…

Say for example, you can make an average of $20 NET per book (easy to do). Based on the above cost figures you will have to sell between 19 and 140 books to cover your initial costs, including annual registration fees wherever applicable.

The high end of the cost range above is really an extreme as far as I'm concerned. For example, it includes $1,000 to write a sales page. If you've written a book, surely you can write your own sales page using any one of hundreds of good models available (See page 93).

Compare this with just the up-front printing costs to do an initial printing of 2,000 copies of a 150 page paperback book at about $2.50 each, under the traditional book publishing model. That's $5,000 plus for the traditional model.

IMPLEMENTATION CHECKLIST

This implementation checklist is a tool designed to help you plan and/or keep track of your progress when implementing the 17 Action Steps detailed in this book.

When you've got all the items checked off it will mean that you have a book/ebook that is on sale through: your own website (as an ebook), and through a digital fulfillment distributor (digital download and POD versions).

ACTION STEPS/SPECIFIC TASKS	PAGE REF.	START DATE	COMPLETE DATE	STATUS √ OR %
Step 1: Research	50			
Demand/supply analysis	50			
Benchmark competition	54			
Step 2: Title	57			
Keyword research	57			
Finalize title	60			
Step 3: Registrations	61			
Register Copyright	61			
Obtain ISBN	62			
Step 4: Domain Name	64			
Finalize domain name	64			
Register domain name	65			
Step 5: Cover/Web Site Artwork	67			
Choose designer	67			
Visualize concept	68			
Approve cover/web site	68			
Step 6: Key Book Parameters	71			
Decide on length, format, etc	71			
Set-up book template	72			

ACTION STEPS/SPECIFIC TASKS	PAGE REF.	START DATE	COMPLETE DATE	STATUS √ OR %
Step 7: Table of Contents	75			
Develop draft TOC	75			
Step 8: Detailed Content	79			
Develop detailed contents	79			
Step 9: Writing the Book/eBook	81			
Write first draft	81			
Step 10: Edit/Revise the	83			
Get 3rd party comments	83			
Do own final editorial review	83			
Do final edits/revisions	83			
Step 11: Create/Publish eBook	86			
Create PDF file(s)	86			
Create any bonus files	87			
Step 12: Create Sales-Mini-Site	90			
Set-up hosting account	92			
Write sales copy for Web	93			
Set-up payment processing	95			
Design, create, upload Web	98			
Step 13: Launch Book/eBook	101			
Obtain testimonials	101			
Make initial special offers	103			
Step 14: Announce Book/eBook	106			
Register in free SEs	106			
Register at pay-per-includes	108			
Initial pay-per-click	108			
Issue news/press release	114			
Step 15: Marketing Book/eBook	115			
Write initial article(s)	115			

ACTION STEPS/SPECIFIC TASKS	PAGE REF.	START DATE	COMPLETE DATE	STATUS √ OR %
Set-up initial joint ventures	117			
Set-up affiliate program	122			
Set-up initial eZine ad	125			
Decide on other marketing	126			
Step 16: Digital Fulfillment	133			
Select digital fulfillment	136			
Submit digital download	139			
Step 17: Print-on-Demand Model	143			
Select POD fulfillment	143			
Obtain additional artwork	145			
Submit files, artwork for	146			

Implementation Checklist Notes:

• The Implementation Checklist is designed so that you can use it both as a planning tool and a progress status tool.

• For example, you can use the *Start/Complete Date* columns to lay out your implementation schedule at the beginning of your book/ebook project.

• Then, as you proceed you can use the *Complete Date* column to record your actual completion dates when a task is done.

• In the *Status* column you can either show a percentage completion (**%**) as you go along, or simply check off a task (√) when it's done.

Further to what I mentioned in the Introduction; if you follow the 17 Action Steps laid out in this book, and use this checklist as your guide, you should be able to complete the entire process in 25 to 30 days if you give it your full-time attention.

MY FAVORITE "HOW-TO" EBOOKS

In the years since I'v been online I have purchased probably 25 or more different eBooks to help guide me in my quest to write, publish and market my ebooks and books online.

At an average cost of, say US $50, that works out to $1,000 or more that I've spent self-educating online.

Of course, that's only part of the story when I start counting the dozens of other information products and services I've downloaded and experimented with along the way. It's all part of the necessary learning curve.

Below is my Top 5 List of "how-to" eBooks that I have used personally, and feel comfortable with recommending to readers of this ebook.

33 Days to Online Profits
By Yanik Silver and Jim Edwards
http://www.33daystoonlineprofits.com
As far as I'm concerned, this is one of the best "how-to" values you can get online. It's a step-by-step walkthrough on how you can develop and set-up your own money-making sales-mini-site in just over a month. You can get the basic eBook very cheap, or upgrade to a more expensive video version.

eBook Secrets – How To Create & Sell Your Own Profitable eBook On The Web
By Ken Silver
http://www.kensilver.com
Back in 2001 this comprehensive "how-to" ebook was the main guide I used to develop my very first ebook. This all-encompassing ebook covers just about everything you need to know, in detail. Another great ebook value.

Instant Internet Profits
By Yanik Silver

http://www.instantinternetprofits.com

When I bought this one back in 2001 it was a step-by-step "how-to" eBook that I found very helpful. I now see that it's since been upgraded to a full-blown course that is fairly pricey. I suggest you try *33 Days To Online Profits* first and then think about upgrading to this one.

Make Your Site Sell! – The Definitive Work On Making Any Web Site Sell
By Ken Evoy, M.D.

http://myss.sitesell.com/

This is considered by many to be the "bible" on the overall subject of Internet Marketing. It's an extensive resource book that covers just about anything you could ever think of on the Internet marketing subject. An excellent reference resource.

How To Promote Your Product – 24 Power Keys Guaranteed To Promote Any Product (or service) On The Net, At Any Time!
By Michael Green

http://www.howtopromoteaproduct.com

I find that this one contains a good summary of just about every marketing and promotion technique that one can use to promote a product and/or website. Even though I was aware (and already using) most of the techniques presented, I still found a few new ones that I've since implemented.

I know there are many other helpful "how-to" ebooks out there. Some of them I've read and others I've decided not to purchase for one reason or another.

I suppose I chose the above ebooks in particular because they tend to emphasize the step-by-step, practical hands-on approach that I've always found the most helpful.

ONLINE PUBLISHING RESOURCES

I believe that if you faithfully follow ALL of the advice and information included in this eBook you will be successful in writing, publishing and marketing your own quality book and/or ebook online.

Nevertheless, even given all the information provided here, there will be some people who won't feel entirely confident until they check out every possibility. So, they will continue to look for additional help and advice.

To save those people a lot of time and trouble I have spent many hours researching what additional online resources are out there that one may want to consult.

When I did a www.google.com search on the term "digital publishing", over 4,490,000 results were returned. For "ebook publishing" it was 219,000 results. And "print-on-demand book" over 55,000 results came back.

So, to get that list down to a meaningful number of sites, I did a detailed review of the first 50 to 100 results from each search and then chose the ones I consider to be the most relevant and useful out of those.

I then listed those sites ranked in order of popularity according to their alexa.com traffic ratings on the day that I conducted this research. Alexa is a respected Web site ranking service that computes traffic rankings by analyzing the Web usage of millions of Web users (See Step 1).

For a subject like "digital publishing" the Alexa ranking, which is based largely on volume of traffic, can be considered a reasonable indicator of quality content.

As you can imagine, researching and compiling these short-lists of links took many tedious hours, so please take advantage of the fruits of my labors.

TOP 35 ONLINE RESOURCES

The following links are what I consider to be **the top 35 online publishing resource and information sites** to help you find any additional resources you feel you may need to help you in developing and publishing your book or ebook online.

As mentioned above, the sites are **ranked in order of popularity according to their alexa.com traffic ratings** on the day that I conducted this research.

Please note that at the time this research was conducted and these lists were compiled, all links were tested and were in good working order.

Ebook Resources

Adobe – eBookmall: If you're looking for the latest eBooks and digital editions ...
http://www.adobe.com/epaper/**ebooks**/ebookmall/

Powell's Books and eBooks: For reading on all types of devices...
http://www.powells.com/**ebooks**tore/**ebooks**.html

EBook Publisher: Makes it easy to publish an eBook ...
http://www.iuniverse.com/

eLibrary Open Ebooks Directory of most ebooks, sold on the Internet.
http://www.e-library.net/

eBook Publishing: The quickest and easiest way to earn a substantial income online
http://www.ebookdirectory.com/ebook_publishing.html

Jogena's eBook Directory: Ebooks are great sources of information**...**
www.jogena.com/ebookdir/ebookdata.htm

Write Create & Promote a Best Seller! In-depth info about how to ...
http://www.fictionfactor.com/order.html

Over 2,400 unique ebook titles in our directory (almost 400 for free)…
http://www.mindlikewater.com

EBookGraphics: No matter what you do, you can write and publish an ebook!
http://www.ebookgraphics.com/

EBook Educational Site where you can read, submit, find free ebooks….
http://www.ebook88.com/

Ebook Publishing Tools: Everything you need to successfully write, publish…
http://www.ebook-publishing-tools.com/

EBookPalace.com: Visitor submitted directory with hundreds of books/eBooks…
http://www.ebookpalace.com/

Knowledge Download: eBook Self Publishing solutions…
http://www.knowledge-download.com

Ebook Publishing: How to Determine if You Should Publish an eBook…
http://www.selfpublishebooks.com/ebook-publishing.html

Ebooks Cafe: Bringing you a wide assortment of books and ebooks…
http://www.ebookscafe.writergazette.com/books.php

Electronic Book Web: Writing an eBook - Your Way to Success!
http://www.ebookweb.com/stories/

POD Resources

Self Publish Books: Learn More About CafePress.com Publishing…
http://www.cafepress.com/cp/info/sell/books.aspx

Lightning Source – The Power of One: We Are On Demand…
http://www.lightningprint.com/

On-Demand Book Publishing: Lulu.com for Authors…
http://www.lulu.com/

Print on Demand Book Publishing: How to Start a POD Publishing Business…
http://www.fonerbooks.com/cornered.htm

On Demand Publishing, Print On Demand Self Publishing **…**
http://www.authorhouse.com/AboutUs/SelfPublishing.asp

Self Publishing Packages - Print On Demand - Publishing Services …
http://www.iuniverse.com/packages/

Warnings and Cautions for Writers--The Truth About **POD Publishing…**
http://www.sfwa.org/beware/printondemand.html

Writing World: Ten Questions to Ask Before You Sign that POD Contract…
http://www.writing-world.com/publish/lick.shtml

BookSurge: Complete POD publishing, fulfillment and distribution services
http://www.booksurge.com

Self Publishing a Book with Print On Demand Publishing Service**…**
http://www2.xlibris.com/pubservices/ps_pubkit.asp

InstantPublisher.com: Custom print on demand book publishing software…

http://www.instantpublisher.com

Distribution methods of POD publishing services…

http://www.poddymouth.wordpress.com/

National Writers Union Print on Demand Publishing report…

http://www.nwu.org/nwu/?cmd=showPage&page_id=1.3.13.10

Publishing Basics… for the self publisher » Vanity & POD Publishing…

http://www.publishingbasics.com/category/vanity-**pod**-**publishing**/

Infinity Publishing: Book publisher, king of print on demand …

http://www.infinitypublishing.com/printondemand.htm

Print-On-Demand: Is a revolutionary, economical new publishing system…

http://www.authorsonline.co.uk/

Which Self Publishing POD Company is Right for You?…

http://www.book-publishers-compared.com/

Print On Demand Quotes: POD quotes from Print On Demand printers

http://www.printquoteusa.com/printers/Print_On_Demandprinting.html

Review: Print-On-Demand Book Publishing: To learn more about POD…

http://www.bainvestor.com/Print-on-demand-book-publishing-review.html

Self Publishing a Book with Print On Demand Publishing Service…

http://www2.xlibris.com/pubservices/ps_pubkit.asp

INDEX

NOTES

NOTES

Lightning Source UK Ltd.
Milton Keynes UK
25 November 2010

9 780978 170080